Africa's Moment

Africa's Moment

PETE ONDENG

Project54Tour
535 West 34th Street
New York, NY 10001

Asset Capital Ltd.
P.O. Box 18061-00100
Nairobi, Kenya

Printed by Lulu.com

Cover design and typesetting by Midas Productions

Photos provided by Project54Tour

"The Road Not Taken" by Robert Frost, from *The Norton Anthology of Modern Poetry*, 2nd ed., New York: W. W. Norton &Co., 1988.

ISBN: 978-0-6152-2190-8

Asset Capital Ltd.
P.O. Box 18061-00100
Nairobi, Kenya

To
David and Betty Ann Whitson of Texas,
with lots of love

Contents

Acknowledgments

I would like to express thanks to my friends and colleagues for their tolerance, affection, and generosity of spirit. Their advice, which sometimes took the form of acutely productive disagreement, served to strengthen this book. Special thanks to Charles Kasing'a, Ezra Mbogori, Kirabo Lukwago, Dan Ole Shani, Wilfred Mlay, Gert van Maanen, Zanele Mbeki, Alice Bomett, Mr. and Mrs. Jan van Haarten, Dr. Helmut Danner and the Hanns-Seidel-Stiftung, and Dr. Tom Costello, all of whom made valuable contributions.

I would especially like to thank my wife and good friend, May, for running the full distance with me.

And finally, to Nan Newell, editor at Word Association Publishers, I owe my heartfelt thanks for her creative inspiration and editorial skill.

Preface

Sometime in early 2000, I was invited to deliver a talk at an international workshop on rural microfinance. The one-day workshop was organized by the International Agricultural Center in collaboration with Wageningen Agricultural University in the Netherlands. At the end of the day, one of the participants, a Dutch lecturer at the university, offered me some interesting feedback.

"That was a typical African speech," he said. I looked at the gentleman quizzically, and he seemed happy to elaborate.

"That was what we refer to as a 'heart on the tongue' speech," he explained. "I think most of us were expecting a bit more of a technical speech with some statistics and maybe some new ideas coming from your experience as a practitioner. Your talk was very much about your personal feelings." The man went on to express how surprised he was at my willingness to be candid to the point of *vulnerability* in front of such an academic crowd.

I thought about the gentleman's remarks for some time, eventually conceding that I could have perhaps been less opinionated in my presentation. Speaking from the heart is always a risky enterprise, and the easiest thing to do in such situations is to block all personal convictions and completely remove oneself from the topic.

During the mental preparations that I underwent before launching into the writing of this book, I had to choose between delivering my message from the heart or from the head. In the end, I decided on my heart. *Africa's Moment* is a personal statement of my belief in a positive future for Africa. The book does not offer easy answers to the myriad of complex social, political, environmental, and economic problems that confront Africa. Africa's problems are not only numerous, but most of them have their roots in a history that is as complex as the problems themselves.

In this book I share some personal, heartfelt convictions about the continent with which I find my identity so intrinsically intertwined. Africa is not some removed subject that I can dissect without cutting my own self open. I find it difficult to talk about Africa without talking about myself. For I am, in a way, the subject. For better or for worse, I am inseparable from the continent. If Africa is in crisis, I am in crisis.

Every time I point an accusing finger, I find the finger pointing back at me as the culprit, the problem, and strangely, even the solution. When I search for whom to blame for our woes, I find that I cannot absolve myself from at least part of the blame. When I ask who holds the key to Africa's escape from the dungeon of poverty and backwardness, I find, to my great surprise, that the key is in my hand. And whenever I have dared to ask the troubling question, "Does anybody out there really care?", the answer has come bouncing back to me like an echo: "How much do *you* care?"

But is there really a future of hope for Africa or am I wasting my breath? Are there enough valid reasons to believe that in the coming decades Africa will rise up from its straw mat and become a better place in which to live than it is today? Will our children grow up to be proud of their African heritage?

The answers to these troubling questions are not easy. Yet there are only two possible answers: yes or no. "*Yes,* there is hope for a positive future for Africa," or "*No,* Africa faces a hopeless future not worth living for." To believe or not to believe in the future, that is the question as well as the fundamental choice before us. For it is in that choice that reality will be created.

The road to Africa's awakening will not open up to us by trying to solve yesterday's problems, but in first accepting that our history is sealed. No people can ever return to their past, no matter how much they may want to do so. We can only derive value from hindsight if we have faith that the future is worth living for.

We need to put on a new mind if we are to succeed in our search for solutions. As Albert Einstein said, "The significant problems we face today cannot be solved at the same level of thinking we were at when we created them."[1]

My prayer is that this book will challenge you to seize the many opportunities that you have to use your time, your talents, and your resources for positive change in Africa.

CHAPTER ONE

The Road I Traveled

Two roads diverged in a wood, and I—
I took the one less traveled by,
And that has made all the difference.
— *Robert Frost*

The date was August 20, 1978. I was nineteen years old then, and just out of high school. The events of that unseasonably chilly morning still stand out vividly in my mind. I had not slept a wink the whole night, and I remember feeling as if I were in some kind of dream.

My mother reached out to hug me, and I noticed there were tears in her eyes. She looked at me sadly and whispered something that I didn't quite grasp, but I nodded all the same. Whatever it was that she couldn't say was written in her eyes. I knew that she loved me and that she would miss me.

I put on a brave face as I bade farewell to each of my seven brothers and sisters. My father was the last to say goodbye to me, and I remember the discomfort I felt as I noticed that he, too, was close to tears. I looked steadily at him as he gave me his parting shots of advice. I knew I would miss him—perhaps more than I would miss anybody else. More than a father, he had become a good friend to me. He gave me a quick hug, and then he told me to move on quickly.

Within minutes I would be boarding the Pan Am flight that would carry me for the first time out of Africa. I was on my way to the United States where I would end up spending the next eight years of my life.

The opportunity to travel to the United States was an unanticipated and unmerited gift born out of one of the saddest experiences in my short life. It was an unexpected twist following the tragic death of my closest childhood friend, an American missionary kid named Clark Whitson. Completely unknown to me, Clark's parents, knowing the deep bond of friendship that had existed between their late son and me, had decided that they would finance my university education in the United States. They had resolved as a family that the money they had set aside over the years for Clark's university education would now go to me. In receiving the gift, I recognized the awful price that had been paid for me to have the chance to move forward in life.

As I made my way across the Atlantic Ocean that August day in 1978, I knew that a new world was about to open up for me. I also knew only too well that I would have to make the most of the opportunity that I had been given to study abroad.

Little did I know, however, that the period of my departure would coincide with a major transitional moment for my country, Kenya. Somewhere between the time that I had bidden my family farewell and the time I arrived in the United States, our president, Jomo Kenyatta, the first and only president Kenya had ever had, had died. Yes! Kenyatta, the larger-than-life figure who had dominated Kenyan politics from even before my birth, had slipped quietly into eternity and left behind a question mark that, for the next few months, would hang ominously over Kenya like a heavy thundercloud waiting to burst open.

At first my mind refused to believe it. So unthinkable was the dying of the president that a law had been passed just a few years earlier declaring it treasonable to even speak of his possible death. And now he was dead. Oh Lord, I remember thinking, the future was about to begin.

Kenyatta's death was a significant milestone, especially for those of us who had been too young to have experienced life during the colonial years. For us, Kenyatta was the embodiment of our history, his political life always having been presented as the starting point of our history as a nation. He was the champion of our independence from British colonial rule, or so we had been taught, and it was this independence that was to have ushered in for us the opportunity to grow and to prosper unfettered by the yoke of colonialism.

At the time of his death, I was yet to learn just how disappointing the post-independence years had turned out to be. Life had somehow shielded me from the realities of our continent. Unknown to me, we were already in a tailspin that would pick up speed and eventually land Africa in a precarious position.

Learning the American Dream

As a student in a virtually all-white university, my being an African proved to be neither an asset nor a liability. Despite our cultural differences, I managed to assimilate myself into the world of my American friends and college mates with little problem. Yet it was in that period that I first came face to face with my identity, not only as an African, but also as a *black* African.

My eyes were open wide. This was America. The land of the free. The home of the brave. The land of milk and honey. The place where dreams supposedly come true. I wanted it all. In my youthful zest, I yearned to experience the things that make America tick. My first big chance came at the end of my first full year of college.

During the last week of the semester—just about the time when students begin to worry about what they will do to earn money during the long summer break—one of the older students invited me to an evening meeting that he himself would be attending. The meeting turned out to be a recruitment meeting where, for about an hour, a man skillfully presented what he referred to as the "opportunity of a lifetime."

"How would you like to travel this summer to meet hundreds of people, and earn between $3,000 and $10,000?" This was how the pitch began. It was one of the most compelling sales pitches my innocent ears had ever heard. I bit the bait. By the end of the evening, I had signed up to join an army of students from across the United States who would soon be converging in Nashville, Tennessee, for an intensive one-week training in the art of direct sales. The company behind the recruitment drive was a publishing company that did virtually all of its business through college students during the three or four months of the summer holidays.

The long road trip to Nashville from Texas was enjoyable in the company of three other students who had signed up for the first time to join the program. We arrived in Nashville late in the evening, some hours after the training was supposed to have begun. We were both excited and nervous as we headed across the grounds of the training center to the big hall where we were to join some three thousand other students from across the nation, many of whom were returning for their second, third, or even fourth year.

During the week that I would spend in training, we worked hard. We studied volumes of material covering sales techniques that work. We memorized our sales pitches; we studied our products and practiced our presentations again and again. In between all of this, we listened to motivational speeches as well as powerful testimonials from students who had been there before.

Beyond the invaluable skills that I would acquire from structured training in the how-to's of selling, I encountered for the first time the substance behind what so many people refer to as the American Dream. True, there was a lot of hype and a lot of what I considered motivational brainwashing, but underlying it all were some basic principles of success that are as true for an individual as they are for a nation of people.

One of these principles that stands out particularly strongly in my mind is the principle of *positive expectation*. This little poem, simple as it is, perhaps carries the essence of the message much better than I could explain it:

If you think you're beaten, you are
If you think you dare not, you don't
If you'd like to win but you think you can't
It's almost certain you won't.

If you think you'll lose, you're lost
For out in this world we find
Success begins with a person's will
It's all in the state of mind.
If you think you're outclassed, you are
You've got to think high to rise
You've got to be sure of yourself before
You can ever win a prize.
Life's battles don't always go
To the stronger or faster man
But soon or late, the one who wins
Is the one who thinks he can. [2]

When the training week ended, we said goodbye to each other and, in groups of two or three, headed for our respective territories where we would be spending the rest of the summer walking from door to door with the mission of getting rich by selling as many books as possible.

My assignment was to a place called Winston-Salem, North Carolina. As I headed out of Nashville with my two colleagues on the Greyhound bus, our heads pumped full of the most positive information I had ever run across, I had no idea that I was about to face the most negative chapter of my American experience. I was about to enter headfirst into a world where who I was would have less to do with the content of my character than with the color of my skin.

On the third day of what was already beginning to feel like an impossible job, I was confronted by the police on the streets of Winston-Salem and bundled into the city jail. There I ended up spending seven long days and nights in a dirty, crowded cell with eleven other men.

My crime, I came to realize, was being black and in the wrong side of town. Apparently, some lady had called the police with claims that I had broken into her house.

For those seven days, I felt abandoned and lonely. The company that had taken me in with such open arms suddenly didn't know me. My relationship to them, they told the police, was that of an independent agent. I was not their employee. Sorry, there was nothing they could do to help. The two other guys with whom I had traveled to North Carolina claimed to have not received the message that I left at the motel where we were sharing a room.

I am not sure how far this whole ordeal would have gone had it not been that the lady who had filed the charges did not show up for the hearing, resulting in the case being dropped. I walked out of the Winston-Salem courthouse feeling angry and confused. By then, the high that I had felt after the week in Nashville was fast fading.

With a cold cup of coffee in my hand, I sat in a lonely corner of a small fast-food restaurant down the street from the jail, wondering if the principles of success were the same for me as for the thousands of other, mostly white students who would be spending that summer peddling their books. It was a pivotal moment for me. I could choose to allow the discouragement of the experience to break me, or I could choose to continue seeing myself as a winner. For reasons that I cannot explain, I chose to continue believing. Despite the bitter experience, I decided then that my success in life would depend less on what other people thought about me, and more on what I thought about myself.

To Stay or To Go

My years in college passed by quickly, and eventually I did manage to finish my studies and even attain professional qualification in my chosen field of finance. My career started off as well as I could have hoped, with three years of ground-level, professional experience with McDonald's Corporation, one of America's best-known businesses. My future with the company looked not only secure, but highly promising.

So it was in early October 1985 that my boss, an African American gentleman, called me into his office for a private chat. The corporation, he explained to me, was under pressure to step up its affirmative-action program. Accusations had been leveled against the company for having so few women, Hispanics, and blacks in its senior ranks. In response to these accusations, the corporation had decided to select a number of promising "minorities" within the organization to be placed on a "fast track" development program that could see a number of them taking up senior posts in the next few years.

"I have recommended you for this program," he said to me. The blank expression on my face must have come as a surprise to him. This was the big break that so many people hoped for, and yet here I was looking glum and confused. I expressed my gratitude to the man for his kind consideration and left the meeting with my emotions in turmoil.

And then the questions began to swirl in my mind. Would I, like so many other foreign students I knew, choose to remain in the United States and turn my back on my home, or would I break away from the good life I had found to go back to the uncertainties of the Third World? It was a question that even today confronts thousands of Africans living in diaspora.

Many years later I would come to realize just how much the so-called brain drain has impacted on Africa's backwardness. According to some estimates, up to 80,000 highly qualified Africans—doctors, lawyers, architects, scientists, and other professionals—leave their countries yearly in search of employment in Europe or North America. The growing emigration problem has left the continent poorer and has become one of the greatest obstacles to Africa's development.

Reversing this exodus is not a simple matter, and I would hate to trivialize it. Many Africans who have gone abroad to study and never returned have done so for legitimate reasons.

Nevertheless, to stay or to go is a choice that most Africans do not have. For the majority, the only choice is to stay and endure the hardships that life offers them within the walls of a prison of hopelessness. Whatever my own motivations at the time, I made a conscious decision that I would return home. Two weeks after my conversation with my boss, I handed in my resignation, and I began to wind up my eight years in the Land of Plenty.

From Trade to Aid

Faced with the options of working for a large accounting firm in Nairobi, my hometown, or accepting an attractive offer from a bilateral donor organization, I chose the latter for no good reason other than the higher salary they offered to me. From one perspective, this was a simple, straightforward, logical decision. In retrospect, however, I can see how that one decision set me on a completely new journey for which I was ill prepared. It was then that I entered the field known widely as "development." For the better part of the next two decades, the word *development* would permeate my language, my plans, my activities, and even my world view. I would end up devoting virtually all of my working energy to the pursuit of the seemingly elusive goal of development.

The concept of development was not completely new to me. Throughout my life, I had heard from parents, teachers, and politicians that our primary objective as Africans was to pursue development. When I left home after high school to pursue my studies overseas, I was told that I should make good use of the opportunity to gain knowledge and then return home to participate in "developing" our nation (or "nation building," as many people referred to it back then).

As a writer and a researcher I confess to having made numerous contributions to beautifully bound papers on development topics. As a public speaker I have participated in more development seminars and conferences than I care to remember.

It is against this background of acquired experience and knowledge in the field of development that I would later stop to ask a simple question: What in the world is this thing called development? If development is to be our ultimate goal as Africans, then what exactly do we mean by it? What specifically are we trying to develop into, and what are the benchmarks or means of measuring our progress toward that noble goal? For as somebody once said, "If you don't know where you are going, any road will get you there."

In my search, I discovered that the concept of development as a worldwide preoccupation began in 1949 when U. S. President Harry S. Truman, in his inaugural speech, announced a massive new program to "develop the underdeveloped countries." The essence of Truman's philosophy was that by investing in countries that were deemed to be underdeveloped and by offering them technical and economic aid, they would be enabled to advance toward "ultimate prosperity."[3]

The idea was unprecedented. Even the expression "underdeveloped countries" was new. It was virtually unknown as a technical term in economics before Truman's speech.

Despite many counter-arguments that scholars have raised about the soundness of the idea, the concept of developing the underdeveloped has dominated international economics for half a century. Say "development" and virtually anyone will imagine a process through which the poor countries "catch up" with the rich ones.

This objective of closing the income gap between rich and poor countries has spawned the creation or redesign of institutions such as the World Bank, specialized United Nations agencies, regional development banks, bilateral aid agencies in the governments of the most advanced economies, and innumerable foundations, research centers, and non-governmental organizations (NGOs). Yet, as far as I can see of all the trends in Africa and elsewhere in the so-called Third World, the global gap between rich and poor countries has not closed. Instead, it continues to widen at an ever-accelerating pace.

In the cold light of statistics, Africa's economic growth has failed to keep up with population increases; exports have declined in relative and absolute terms; food production has dropped off; imports of food and other necessities have risen greatly; import substitution industries have not lived up to expectations; industrialization has, with some exceptions, failed to materialize; borrowing and debt have soared; currencies have weakened or collapsed; state revenues have plummeted; state-controlled economic activities have foundered; state-funded services have declined or disintegrated; and official economies have shrunk while parallel economies have grown.

So today the outside world looks at Africa not just as an economic failure, but also as an area in which it is fruitless to invest and with which it is better not to trade. Because of Africa's political instability, foreign investors consider it unwise to become involved in any long-term productive activities. Short-term profit considerations prevail, reinforcing a situation in which Africans themselves are reluctant to invest in their own countries. Instead, they seek quick profits, often to be hoarded abroad.

What all these sorry statistics tell us is that, despite the fads, fancies, new techniques, new directions and endless policy rethinks that have characterized the development business over the last half-century, and despite the expenditure of hundreds of billions of dollars, there is little evidence to prove that the poor of the Third World, much less Africa, have actually benefited. The question that immediately comes to my mind then is this: Is it in spite of development aid that African economies have suffered so much loss, or could it be that the aid itself is part of the problem that has stood in the way of our progress? I will come back to this question in a later chapter.

For me, the real picture of Africa is only beginning to come into focus. Over the past few years I have had the opportunity to see and interact with the continent from a perspective that was much broader and deeper than I had previously experienced. From Senegal to South Africa, I have had the opportunity to get glimpses of an Africa that few Africans will ever get the chance to see.

Whether it was walking through cocoa plantations in Ghana or sharing a meal under a tree with peanut farmers in Zimbabwe, I have had the opportunity to drink in the beauty of Africa, and I have wished that I could put it in a bottle and share it with the rest of the world. Through it all, I have come to believe more than ever that the real African story is one that will never be told or even written about. It is a story that has to be lived and experienced.

But there are two sides to this story. Intertwined in the complexities of our diverse histories, politics, cultures, tribes and religions, there is, on the one side, the story of heaven, beckoning from the distant horizon and pointing to the enormous potential that sits buried in the soul of Africa. On the other side is the story of hell with its wide, gaping mouth waiting to drain all our hopes and dreams down into the ugly cesspool of conflict, poverty, exploitation, and human suffering. In these two stories, I have witnessed a dilemma that cannot be resolved by any amount of wishful thinking or intellectual debate. It is a dilemma that calls for a fundamental change in the way we see ourselves and the world around us.

Few people would dispute the assertion that the so-called development effort has failed. In my view, the failure emanates from the flawed premise on which the very concept of development was first introduced, and on which most contemporary development programs continue to be built: that someone from outside the box can somehow transform the lives of people in the box without actually stepping in the box.

Am I Part of the Solution or Part of the Problem?

A story is told of two men who were having a discussion about the poor. One of them said to the other, "You know, I'd like to ask God a question. "Oh yeah, what would you like to ask Him?" his friend asked. The man replied, "I'd like to ask God why He allows all this pain and poverty and hurting in the world."

"Well, why don't you go ahead and ask Him?" his friend inquired.

"I'm afraid to," he said hesitantly. "I am afraid that God will just turn around and ask me the same question."

This story summarizes the essence of my message in response to the hanging question of what should be done about the social and economic problems that continue to subdue two thirds of the world's inhabitants. Like many others who sit on the outside looking in, I have the luxury of being able to remove myself and even walk away from Africa's problems if I were to so choose. In relative terms, I am, by the grace of God, quite well off. I am literate, I am healthy, and I have had the opportunity to travel to many places around the world.

My children go to good schools, I read books and buy newspapers, and I eat more than I should. I have a computer with e-mail and Internet access, I have a reliable car, a television, and a microwave oven, and I can be reached practically anytime anywhere on my mobile telephone.

Within reason, I choose where to go, what to do, what to see, and whom to meet. I have had the opportunity to develop my talents and interests, and these have widened my world of possibilities and shaped my preferences among life's offers.

So, if I am so fortunate, then why am I not doing more to help those who are so much worse off than I am? Do I need to see more in-depth analyses of poverty by the United Nations to convince me that I should join in the fight? Do I perhaps believe that a more concerted donor effort would be the answer to Africa's liberation from poverty?

Could it be that I consider the task of poverty alleviation to be so much bigger than me that my contribution would not be worth the effort? Could it be that because I have seen so much development aid go to waste and achieve so little, I have become cynical and apathetic? Or could it be that I have simply learned the art of pacifying my conscience by pointing to others who I believe are better placed to make a difference?

These are not easy questions. But they are questions that all those who have anything to say about Africa should first reflect upon before opening their mouths. At the end of my own introspection, I came to the conclusion that it is not the lack of resources or the lack of human capacity, but rather the inherent limitations of human nature that keep Africa bound in the dungeons of deprivation.

I have also come to believe that no amount of money thrown at Africa will solve Africa's problems until both the givers and the takers have a change of heart. If there were a genuine will among those able to help the poor out of their misery, we would most certainly find ways to do so.

CHAPTER TWO

What We Believe

As a man thinketh in his heart, so is he.
—*Proverbs 23:7*

On March 30, 1998, four days before my thirty-ninth birthday, *Time* ran an unusually upbeat, forward-looking cover story entitled "Africa Rising." I remember reading the article with great interest— not so much for its journalistic excellence, but more for the unexpected message of hope that seemed to flow from its pages.

"Hope," the article stated, "is probably Africa's rarest commodity." It went on to say that although this hope may be buried amid the despair that haunts the continent, there now seemed to be more optimism in the air about Africa than there had been in decades.

This story is not about the Africa you think you know. The usual images are painted in darkest colors. At the end of the twentieth century, we are repeatedly reminded, Africa is a nightmarish world where chaos reigns. Nothing works. Poverty and corruption rule. War, famine, and pestilence pay repeated calls. The land, air, water are raped, fouled, polluted. Chronic instability gives way to lifelong dictatorships. Every nation's hand is out, begging aid from distrustful donors. Endlessly disappointed, 740 million people sink into hopelessness....[However] ...out of sight of our narrow focus on disaster, *another Africa is rising, an Africa that works....*[4]

The article astounded me. Why would *Time*, a prestigious and internationally respected news magazine, come out with such a strong message of hope for Africa when the rest of the world was reeling from the shock of destabilized global financial markets? I recall so distinctly that 1998 was a year in which the whole world seemed to be groaning from the effects of one of the greatest economic catastrophes of modern times. Most of eastern Asia, including Japan, was in deep recession. Indonesia's gross domestic product (GDP) was expected to fall that year by as much as fifteen percent, and by six to seven percent in South Korea and Thailand. And it wasn't just Asia. Russia's government had defaulted on its debt, and its economic predicament was worsening almost by the day.

Even some developed economies, such as those of Britain and Canada, were slowing. Wall Street had fallen sharply from its peak with tumbling share prices shrinking the world's financial wealth by billions of dollars. The sickness had spread far and wide, and as far as my simple eyes could see, Africa was not exempted.

The *Time* article was beautiful prose, to say the least. Deep down, I wanted to believe it. I wanted to accept that the future of Africa would be different from its past. In the secrecy of my thoughts, I allowed myself the space to dream, to wonder if maybe, just maybe, Africa was destined to always travel in the opposite direction from the rest of the world. Could it be, unlikely as it was, that as the rest of the world spiraled out of control, this could truly be Africa's turn to rise? Was this the appointed time for our wheels of fortune to begin turning?

Having grown accustomed to endless prophesies of doom about Africa, I found the *Time* cover story to be surprising but certainly refreshing reading. Encouraging as it was, however, the story provoked in me an intense anxiety about what lay ahead for Africa and its seven hundred million or so people.

The timing of the *Time* article did not escape my notice: U. S. President Bill Clinton was about to make his much-heralded trip to Africa. During that six-nation tour, President Clinton would speak warmly of African successes. "One hundred years from now," he said, "your grandchildren and mine will look back and say, this was the beginning of a new African renaissance."

President Clinton's remarks were in reference to a fledgling movement that had been born out of the inspiration of Thabo Mbeki, then deputy president of South Africa under Nelson Mandela. Earlier that year, Mbeki had opened a highly publicized African renaissance conference in Johannesburg where he had challenged Africans to seize the moment and take hold of their future. "The new African world which the African renaissance seeks to build is one of democracy, peace and stability, sustainable development and a better life for people, non-racism and non-sexism, equality among the nations, and a just and democratic system of international governance."[5] Mkebi's speech was as inspiring as it was challenging.

Like many other grand ideas that had come before it, the African renaissance movement would end up being short-lived. For that brief moment, however, it served as a rallying point for idealists like myself who wished to see magic falling down from the sky and transforming Africa into a new reality of prosperity and peace.

A Rude Awakening

If the *Time* article induced me to search my soul, it was yet another blazing magazine cover story that would motivate me two years later to take action. The date was May 13, 2000. The magazine was none other than the influential *Economist*.

"The Hopeless Continent!" screamed the headline from the newsstand. I remember the knot I felt in my stomach as I picked up the magazine and walked over to the cashier to pay for it. *The Economist* was brutal in its assessment of Africa:

> Floods in Mozambique; threats of famine in Ethiopia
> (again); mass murder in Uganda; the implosion of Sierra
> Leone; and a string of wars across the continent. The new
> millennium has brought more disaster than hope to Africa.
> Worse, the few candles of hope are flickering weakly....
> The next generation [of Africans] will be more numerous,
> poorer, less educated, and more desperate....[6]

The article sneered at the talk of an African renaissance, referring to it as an illusion. "Does Africa have some inherent character flaw that keeps it backward and incapable of development?" it asked. "The figures—not to mention the recent crop of disasters and wars—now suggest that Africa is losing the battle." What a damning conclusion.

The article hit me like a bullet between the eyes. It was barely two years since the publication of the *Time* story, and at first I wondered how a story of hope could be transformed so quickly into one of hopelessness. Unlike the refreshingly positive *Time* article, the *Economist* story was what I had come to expect from the international media. Exposure to this perpetual negativity may explain why the *Time* article took me by surprise.

Like so many other Africans, I had over the years become drenched with the feeling of hopelessness that emanates from being told again and again that ours is a continent that doesn't work, and probably never will. It is a hopelessness that pervades the average African's mind—especially those born into the slavery of poverty—and creates a state of mental poverty devoid of vision, hope, and in many cases, even the energy to survive.

As far back as I can remember, Western journalists, and even our very own writers, have written and spoken about the continent of Africa as a lost cause. The tales of woe have become repetitive and increasingly negative. The message that has become all too familiar, especially to those of us who read and desire to be well-informed, is that if ever there was a hope for Africa, it is no longer there. In short, Africa is a fad that has passed.

The Media vs. Africa

The *Economist* article disturbed me deeply, partly because I knew only too well the power that the Western media had over my own attitude and my perceptions of Africa. It is a power that can manipulate reality and effectively create its own distorted history.

The endless stream of Africa-bashing stories coming from outside usually goes unchallenged by our own thinkers and writers, not because of the sophistication of the arguments that the stories present, but because of the enormous power wielded by the media organizations that market them.

Having lived abroad where I hungered for news from home, I am painfully aware of how little media attention African countries receive in the West except in times of crisis. Even then, the tendency is to accentuate and reinforce the negative images of the continent. Consequently, people from the West are rarely exposed to images of normal, healthy African civilization. The majority of people outside the continent have come to accept hunger, disease, conflict, and death in Africa as quite normal for that part of the world.

During my recent four-year stint in the Netherlands, I could not help but notice the sharp contrast in the manner in which the same media reported the ghastly things that the Serbs were perpetrating against the Kosovars. The debate that was played out in the Western media was about whether or not those ghastly things were normal for that part of the world.

The world looked on in horror and disbelief at the atrocities that were being committed by the Serbs, and questions were raised everywhere as to how this kind of barbarism could actually be happening in Europe. They could not fathom that the Serbs, as Europeans, would be capable of such uncivilized behavior. Something, or someone, out of the ordinary had to be responsible for the horror, and that something or someone had to be removed in order for civilization to return. The rest is history. An American-led NATO force stepped in and dealt decisively with the Milosevic government that was deemed to be behind the atrocities.

Which brings us back to Africa and its sad story. How often do we ever hear non-Africans crying in disbelief, "How can such barbarism be happening in Africa!"? The sad truth is that as long the world continues to hold a *paradigm* of Africa as a no-good place of violence, murder, slaughter and mayhem, any effort by the world community to rescue Africa from its internal enemies would only be seen as a waste of time.

The Power of a Paradigm

Stephen R. Covey, author of *The Seven Habits of Highly Effective People*, makes a compelling argument about the power of paradigms, and how our paradigms effectively control our lives.

The word *paradigm* comes from the Greek. It was originally a scientific term and is more commonly used today to mean a model, theory, perception, assumption, or frame of reference. In the more general sense, it is the way we "see" the world—not in terms of our visual sense of sight, but in terms of perceiving, understanding, and interpreting.[7]

In explaining the concept of paradigms, Covey uses an example that I have found helpful in my own effort to explain what I believe is one of Africa's greatest dilemmas: Suppose you wanted to arrive at a specific location in central Chicago. A street map of the city would be a great help to you in reaching your destination. But suppose you were given the wrong map. Through a printing error, the map labeled Chicago was actually a map of Detroit. Can you imagine the frustration of trying to reach your destination?

There are of course several things that you could choose to do. You might decide to work on your behavior—you could try harder, be more diligent, and even double your speed. But your efforts would only succeed in getting you to the wrong place faster. You might then decide to work on your attitude—you could think more positively, for example. But you would still not get to the right place. You would still be lost.

The fundamental problem in this situation would not be your attitude, but simply that you have the wrong map. If you had the right map of Chicago, then diligence would become important, and if you encountered obstacles along the way, your attitude could make a difference. But the first and most important requirement is that you start out with the right map.

Each of us has many, many maps, or paradigms, in our heads. We interpret everything we experience through these mental maps. We seldom question their accuracy. We are usually even unaware that we have them. We simply assume that the way we see things is the way they really are or the way they should be. The tragedy of this is that so many people spend their lives driving around in circles and never getting where they should be going because they picked up the wrong maps along the way.

So what does all this have to do with Africa? My answer is, "Just about everything!" I am convinced that the perception, or paradigm, through which many non-Africans view Africa is one of the key obstacles to Africa's development. Unfortunately, this negative perception is not confined to non-Africans.

Too many Africans carry around a burden of negativity about themselves and their continent that severely cripples their ability to progress. Whether from forces of history or from years of repeated bombardment by the highly negative mass media, Africa has adopted a self-image that feeds on itself and becomes a self-fulfilling prophecy.

In his fascinating little book entitled *Doing Business in Africa*, Chudi Ukpabi points out a number of factors that have influenced the submergence of the African's identity and self-perception. Ukpabi points out, for example, that many Europeans are willing to study the Japanese, Chinese, Indian, and Indonesian languages and ways of life in order to communicate and do business in those societies. Yet the same Europeans generally are unwilling to do the same with regard to African society.

Because of existing power relations, the Africans are the ones pressured into adapting to Western thinking, its language, religion, rules of personal conduct, etc. The African is expected to change his traditional management culture, his organizational and decision-making skills in order to provide a business environment in Africa deemed acceptable by the international community.[8] In other words, in order to succeed even in business, the African has to submerge his own identity and cultivate the Western business culture in order to be considered a good business partner. The damage is subconscious, and its impact is far-reaching.

Years of mental bombardment have resulted in a debilitating, negative self-image that renders social and economic progress almost impossible. It doesn't take a genius to come to the conclusion that the battle for Africa's future will not be won until it is first won in the mind of the African. As much as we find ourselves going through the motions of development, few Africans really believe in their hearts that Africa will ever have the substance to rise out of the mire of poverty and hardship that has only become more pronounced over the years. This, to me, is the real tragedy of Africa.

The Starting Point

I wish I could end this chapter by stating that all the stories propagated by the Western media were lies. I wish I could have been able to argue that the picture painted of a continent steeped in corruption, disease, and strife was the work of a baseless conspiracy cooked up by some racist group bent on bringing down Africa. Writing this book would have been infinitely easier.

Despite the obvious damage caused by the decidedly negative mass media, one reality that we in Africa cannot ignore, even in our desire to accentuate the positive, is that Africa does in fact have some very serious problems. From east to west, north to south, Africa is in desperate need of a new direction. With all the dark clouds hanging above her, Africa stands like a severely disabled child, helplessly watching the coming storm, feeling the bitter cold, but not having the strength or the mind to do anything about it.

No longer is Africa under the bondage of the evil slave trade that ripped asunder her soul, nor is she under the oppression of colonialism that undermined the dignity of her people. Yet her spirit seems to be chained to some invisible post that keeps her walking around in circles while she digs her own grave.

As the rest of the world repositions and redefines itself under the unstoppable forces of globalization, we find ourselves still struggling to come to terms with our identity. This is the painful paradox with which we have become accustomed to living, a paradox which the two contradicting magazine articles represent so well—that latent struggle embedded deep within the soul of every African man and woman who has yearned for a taste of freedom from the prison in which most of us were born.

We Africans have to come to terms with the fact that the responsibility of Africa's future sits squarely on our own shoulders. The time has come for us to examine the foundation on which our future is being built. If the crumbling walls of the continent are the result of a faulty foundation, then we have no choice but to go back to the drawing board and examine in what or whom we will put our trust for the journey that lies ahead. There is no doubt that history repeats itself, and unless the underlying conditions that led to our sad history are altered, we should not be surprised to find ourselves being driven once again into subjugation to the same forces that bound us in the past. In this awakening, we must recognize the power that lies in thought.

> *A group of frogs were traveling through the woods, and two of them accidentally fell into a deep pit. All the other frogs gathered around the pit. When they saw how deep the pit was, they shouted down to the unfortunate frogs that they would never get out.*
>
> *The two frogs ignored the comments and tried to jump up out of the pit. The other frogs kept telling them to stop, that they were as good as dead. Finally, one of the frogs took heed to what the other frogs were saying and simply gave up. He fell down and died.*
>
> *The other frog continued to jump as hard as he could. Once again, the crowd of frogs yelled at him to stop the pain and suffering and just die. The more the other frogs shouted at him to*

stop, the harder he jumped. Finally, to the surprise of everyone, he made it out, whereupon the other frogs gathered around him and asked, "Why did you continue jumping? Didn't you hear us?"

The little frog looked at his companions in bewilderment and explained to them that he had not heard a word they had said. "I am deaf," he said. "When I looked up and saw you shouting at me, I thought that you were encouraging me not to give up, but to keep trying."

The little frog made it out of the pit, not because of what the others said, but in spite of what they said. The moral of the story is that we need to become deaf to the messages of hopelessness that are constantly directed our way. Only then will we ever be able to see our way out of the pit, and to turn that seemingly impossible dream into reality. Africa needs to put on a new mind. She will never move forward until her people decide to close their minds to the disparaging voices of doom that shout down the pit with contempt for everything African.

In the next chapter we will take a closer look at the issues surrounding Africa's state of poverty. Poverty, like any other problem in life, must be understood if it is to be solved.

CHAPTER THREE

The Wretched Poor

There are many people talking about the poor,
but few people are talking to the poor.
—*Mother Teresa*

In the summer of 1997, I had the privilege of participating in a fascinating two-week trip to Bangladesh, where I was exposed to a country classified as one of the poorest in the world. The sight of poverty was not new to me. As an African, I had become accustomed to living in a world immersed in a sea of want. However, being in Bangladesh as a foreigner from a faraway country gave me the opportunity to see poverty from a fresh perspective.

For those two weeks, I stepped into another world. This time, for a change, I was the development tourist coming to peer curiously at the poor of another country as if they were exhibits in an ancient museum. In the villages I visited, I experienced the phenomenon of little children pressing playfully around me to touch my strange-colored skin and my funny-looking hair. The old men in the villages stared at me with open interest while the wives and mothers rushed around to find their special visitor a stool to sit on or a cup of water to drink.

I was moved by the pathetic state of the lives of the Bengali people. Beyond the language barrier that separated me from many of the families with whom I still shared some wonderful moments, I saw real people with real needs. Through it all, I came to appreciate anew the fact that poverty is nondiscriminatory when it comes to race, creed, religion, and nationality. A poor little Bengali child with an infected foot suffers the same pain as a Kenyan or American child in a similar condition. An old woman with nothing in the house to feed her children experiences the same anguish as her counterpart in Africa or the United States.

I returned home to my country with a deeper conviction that *nobody deserves the curse of poverty in a world of such riches.* An even deeper and more disturbing stirring in my spirit, however, was the question of *whether anybody deserves to be rich in a world of so much poverty.*

Understanding Our Poverty

If strife, which we will look at in depth in a later chapter, is the biggest enemy of Africa's long-term development, then poverty is her twin sister. While war and incessant conflict have blinded our eyes and prevented us from *seeing* the road toward our progress, it is our poverty that prevents us from *walking* the road of progress—even where we are able to see. It is because of poverty that Africa sits immobilized like a crippled beggar on a mat by the roadside.

To many people, the word *Africa* is a symbol or even a synonym of the word *poverty.* It is difficult to talk about Africa without at least some mention of its endemic poverty. Africa's poverty is a societal problem on which most people have some opinion, but one whose solution has proven to be as elusive as its definition.

The United Nations Development Program (UNDP), in its definition of poverty, talks about "a denial of choices and opportunities for living a tolerable life." The World Bank is a bit more mechanical, defining a poor person as one whose consumption or income level falls below some predefined minimum, which is usually identified as the "poverty line." Poverty lines vary in time and place, and each country uses lines that are supposedly appropriate to its level of "development," societal norms, and values. Other often-used terms that attempt to stratify the poor are "absolute poverty," "relative poverty," and "the poorest of the poor."

The global preoccupation with the subject of poverty has spawned an industry of researchers and statisticians as well as a plethora of world conferences and forums that seemingly only provide an opportunity for people to *talk* about the extent and measures of this problem. Information on consumption and income is obtained regularly through sample surveys of households which are asked to answer detailed questions on spending habits and sources of income. Such surveys are conducted more or less routinely in most countries. The resulting statistics are usually misleading in their use as measures of the welfare of a nation.

One commonly misused statistic for measuring the welfare of a nation is per capita income. In simple terms, the per capita income of a country is determined by taking the quantifiable income generated by the country and dividing it by the number of people in that country. The deception lies in the implication that individual lives are improved when per capita income goes up. To put it another way, it is often implied that an increase in per capita income means a reduction in poverty. The truth is that an increase in per capita income does not necessarily mean that everyone is better off.

If there is one sure thing that all the surveys do show for Africa, however, it is that the size of the pie that could conceivably be shared, if sharing were the agenda, continues to shrink at an alarming rate. Even if we were to use the very narrow income angle to measure poverty, it becomes quite evident that while other developing nations have made great economic strides over the past thirty years, those in sub-Saharan Africa have steadily staggered backward.

In 1965, the average income of an African, as measured according to the flawed per capita statistics, was equal to fourteen percent of that received by the average person in the Western industrialized world. By

1995, however, the income of the average African had actually shrunk to seven percent of the income of the average Westerner.[9]

Besides all this is the often forgotten reality that poverty in Africa is more than an economic issue. African poverty cuts deep into the very substance of human existence. In comparison to poverty in other regions of the world, the extremes of Africa's poverty are an outrage. The problem is so massive that few dare even to contemplate an entry point into how to solve it.

The Prison of Hopelessness

For lack of hope, many Africans live from one day to the next, grateful if only they can have something to eat and a place to sleep. They dare not think about tomorrow, because tomorrow stares them threateningly in the face, and so they remain hopelessly caged in the present. The view from within these walls is almost unimaginable for those on the outside who look into the cage from a distance and wonder why Africans can't seem to get their act together.

From an outside viewpoint, Africa is the ugly duckling—the unlovable member of the family whose very existence creates endless discomfort and evokes embarrassment, shame, and fear. But for those on the inside, there is only the echo of their own voices as they cry out desperately to be understood as deserving more than the daily rations of crumbs thrown at them with the primary aim of appeasing the conscience of the throwers.

The imagery of imprisonment is very real in my mind, but it took on a particularly strong meaning following a horrific experience I had one day in Nairobi. Not only did this experience cause me to question the principle of human equality, but it provided me with a clearer mental picture of the stark reality of life for the vast majority of Africans. I want to share this story with you.

One day I received news that an acquaintance of mine had "snapped" and had been admitted to Nairobi's Mathare Mental Hospital. Mathare is a place whose very name sends shudders down the spines of most

Kenyans. It is not a place for people with weak stomachs. Like so many public institutions in Africa, the hospital has been rundown from years of neglect and underfunding.

I remember being nervous as I made my way to the institution to see the sick gentleman. At the gate, an attendant offered to guide me to where the patients were kept. It was my first real encounter with the wretchedness of the lives of mental patients in Kenya, and it was something I will never forget. It took everything to keep from turning and running away. The sight of the mental patients locked up like caged animals with no control over their fate was one of the saddest scenes I had ever encountered.

On my way onto the hospital premises, I had noticed a man pushing a wheelbarrow of what I assumed was garbage, but which I later came to learn was the evening meal en route to the pen where the patients would be fed. These patients, I remember concluding, were the lost people of our society. They were the forgotten men and women whose lives had been stripped of all human dignity and hope.

As it turned out, I was not allowed to see the man I had come to see, and I remember later wondering if it had ever really been my desire to see him in that rotten place. I remember trying to leave in a hurry, wanting to get away from there as fast as I could, back to the world that I knew—my air-conditioned world of television, e-mail and other trappings of affluence, back to the world where people's actions are judged by the black and white standards of good and evil, right and wrong.

The world of the insane is a gray world—nothing is black or white. Once a person crosses over that blurred boundary between the normal and the abnormal, he becomes a prisoner of himself—no longer accountable to society for his deeds. It is a scary world to me, a prison where both good people and bad people end up—not because of crimes they have committed, but because of illnesses that few understand, and fewer care to discuss. Mathare is our dumping ground for such people, people whom our society considers to be impaired and who apparently can be legitimately stripped of even their most basic human rights.

As I tried to make my way rapidly from the disturbing scene at Mathare, I was suddenly jolted by the shrill cry of a man calling out after me. I froze in my tracks, and for a brief moment, my eyes locked with his. I will never forget the look on the face of that poor, helpless stranger as he pleaded with me from behind the chain-linked fence not to leave him there. Amidst the raving madness that was swirling around him, the man looked to me as normal as anybody on the outside. And yet there he was, locked up and probably forgotten, even by those who had been so close to him. The attendant tried impatiently to hurry me along, explaining that the man was a crazy nut and that I shouldn't be bothered by his outburst.

This is a sad story without an ending. I left the hospital grounds and never looked back. I will never know what brought that poor man to such a horrible place, and I suppose our paths will never cross again. Yet I am painfully aware of the indelible print that encounter left on my mind as I now consider the poor African looking out at those who walk by, holding their noses and looking the other way, living their own lives in freedom. The poor African is also in a prison, a prison that they will never understand: the prison of poverty.

Blaming the Blameless

Not long after the Mathare Hospital incident, I had the opportunity to share a leisurely Sunday afternoon with a high-ranking official of the Kenyan government with whom I had become closely acquainted. The gentleman was someone whom I had grown to admire and respect, for his public profile was one of unwavering integrity and purposefulness.

"What can we do to lift these poor people out of their misery?" I asked him in the course of a discussion. I was not looking for a pat answer, nor was I looking for some official government position on the matter. This was a private discussion, and I was hoping to hear the personal convictions of a man whom I felt was in a good position to influence the direction of a number of government policies.

The answer I got took me completely by surprise. But it was certainly not an argument that was new to me.

"There is very little that you and I can do for the poor people of Africa," the official said to me with finality in his voice. "The reason Africans are poor is that they are lazy and corrupt," he continued. "We have to teach our people to get themselves out of their own poverty."

Although I did not indicate it then, the gentleman's answer to my question disturbed me deeply. I disagreed with the implication that poor people are poor by choice. This line of thinking is as uninformed as it is unfair. The World Bank and the International Monetary Fund (IMF) have often been quick to blame the poor countries themselves without taking the time to understand the root causes of the failures of their so-called poverty alleviation programs. These organizations espouse the theory that all the problems will be solved if poor countries simply adopt the right policies and follow the advice of rich countries that is dispensed by institutions such as themselves.

I have serious problems with this simplistic argument. *Poor people do not choose to be poor.* Poor people are poor largely because they cannot help but be poor. Rich countries, eager not to be held accountable for poverty in the rest of the world, hold the view that the poor have only themselves to blame for their condition. This argument is as patently wrong as it is insensitive to the plight of the poor.

Dr. Jeffrey Sachs, the world-renowned Harvard economics guru who for years has been a critic of the IMF and the World Bank for their policies regarding developing countries, argues fervently against this notion. He points out that the poor are suffering in large part because of tremendous biological, ecological, and geographical obstacles not faced in rich countries. Tropical countries in particular have several severe disadvantages, including susceptibility to infectious diseases such as malaria, hookworm, sleeping sickness, and schistosomiasis, whose transmission generally depends on a warm climate.

"If it were true that the poor were just like the rich but with less money," Sachs argues, "the global situation would be vastly easier than it is. As it happens, the poor live in different ecological zones, face different health conditions, and must overcome agronomic limitations that are very different from those of rich countries. Those differences, indeed, are often a fundamental cause of persisting poverty."[10]

Clearly, the subject of poverty needs to be elevated above mere statistics. Discussions on poverty should transcend intellectual debate and penetrate to the core of human attitude and behavior. As long as poverty is viewed and discussed from an impersonal angle that does not recognize the intrinsic value of all human life, we can be sure of one thing: the poor will always be with us.

Whatever the estimates of numbers—and whatever the outcome of the endless scholastic arguments about definitions, statistics, and the degree of deprivation—there are so many people who are so poor, the prospect of future misery is so appallingly clear, and present efforts to eliminate the misery are so inadequate that numbers are almost irrelevant in seeing what to do next. So much needs to be done and so many radical changes have to be made that no estimates, however optimistic, could undermine the case for trying to do much more and doing it better and faster.[11]

CHAPTER FOUR

The Threat of AIDS

The child was diseased at birth, stricken with a hereditary ill that only the most vital of men are able to shake off. I mean poverty, the most deadly and prevalent of all diseases.

—*Eugene O'Neill*

Until 1998, AIDS was a topic that I could talk about quite comfortably, though I maintained enough of a distance to be able to switch it off at will and get on with my life. In April of that year, I came face to face for the first time with the ugliness and horror of this plague. I want to open this chapter by sharing with you an incredible story.

During the long Easter holiday weekend of that year, I accompanied my aging father from Nairobi to the tiny, obscure village of Randago in the western part of Kenya. This was the place my father called home. As children growing up in the city, my siblings and I had spent occasional school holidays there with our grandmother, but over the years, my trips to Randago had become more and more like pilgrimages of obligation to the family ties that still existed in that dusty enclave of forgotten humanity. Except for the faces, the village has remained the same—frozen in time, with its mud huts and a marginal existence that has somehow continued against almost insurmountable odds.

For the millions of tourists who flock our game reserves every year, this is the Kenya that they will never get to see. It is the essence of what development aid, as it currently exists, cannot even begin to address. But what I see here among the barefooted, hungry, uneducated children are people with whom I share the bond of kinship: cousins, uncles, and women who think of me as their son.

My father and I arrived at the village late in the afternoon. We would be spending the night in the house that he had built while I was still a child. The very fact that I would be spending a night in my father's house—me, a grown man with his own family—was itself a traditional taboo, but one of many that my family had broken away from. The house was a semi-modern, three-bedroom structure that stood out like a sore thumb in the pathetic surroundings.

We were tired after the long journey. The last five kilometers through the virtually impassable road had only added to the feeling that we were entering a place cut off from the rest of the world. Randago has no electricity, no running water, and no medical facilities. The nearest telephone is about five miles away. As we entered the village, we passed by the school with its mud walls and gaping windows. We could see the children running around barefoot in the dusty playground. This was their world, the place where they would get their bearings and a perspective that would guide them in their future lives.

Except for the grace of God, I thought to myself, this is where I would have spent my life. But life had been kind to me. For no reason that I could boast of, I had escaped the angry clutches of poverty and somehow made it in a world that, for the most part, was oblivious to the plight of these wretched souls.

As usual, our arrival attracted attention, and for many of those who came to greet us, our coming raised hopes of some material handout. Before long, we were brought up to date on the latest news, mostly about who had died and who was sick.

"How is Mariam doing?" my father asked my aunt who had come

in from digging in her little garden to greet us. Her thin, gaunt face was callous from years of endless toil that had taken her nowhere.

I listened carefully as she narrated the horrible ordeal that Mariam had been going through. Mariam was my cousin. We had heard about her condition, which had not been officially diagnosed, but we were almost certain that she was suffering from AIDS. Her husband had died the year before from what the doctor had diagnosed as tuberculosis.

The prognosis of the doctor and the refusal of anyone to even mention the possibility of AIDS did not surprise me. Most AIDS workers say that denial, accompanied by a paralyzing fatalism, is by far the biggest obstacle to their work.[12]

The daylight was beginning to fade, and we decided that we should go to see Mariam before the village was overcome by darkness. Along the way, my father got caught up in a conversation with one of the villagers, so I walked with my aunt down the crooked, overgrown path to the hut where Mariam had been confined for the past few weeks.

A hideous stench engulfed me as I entered the small, round, thatched hut. I reached for the back of a wooden chair that was close at hand to steady myself. As my eyes adjusted to the darkness, I saw the figure draped in a blanket on a bed against the mud wall.

"Mariam, I've brought you a visitor," my aunt said rather loudly. Mariam moved slightly but said nothing. My aunt then excused herself and left me to spend a few precious moments with my sick cousin.

"How are you doing, Mariam?" I asked in my vernacular as I pulled the chair next to the bed. It was a stupid question and I immediately wished I hadn't asked it. I stared helplessly at the bony face and wondered how life could still exist in such a body. Before she could speak, her throat became clutched in racking spasms. She closed her eyes in obvious pain, and her breath came in shallow gasps.

"I am not too bad today," she said in a raspy voice that sent chills down my spine. She talked slowly, and I listened as she explained that she had not eaten anything in a couple of days, and so was not vomiting like before. She was even too weak to go outside to relieve herself.

Despite our family ties, I really did not know Mariam very well. A year had passed since she had left Nairobi and moved back to the village following the death of her husband. From what I understood, she had fallen sick about three months later. Out of the nine months of sickness, she had spent approximately two weeks in the nearest government-run hospital which, for a healthy person, was a good two-hour walk. After the two weeks in which she had had to share a single bed with another sick woman, she was carried back home, essentially to die.

After some twenty minutes of listening to Mariam's harrowing ordeal, I reached out and touched her hand. She clutched my fingers and stared into my face with an intensity that frightened me. My visit with Mariam finally came to an end, and I pulled away and staggered drunken-like out of the hut into the fresh air outside. My mind swirled with pity, shock, disgust, and confusion. For thirty minutes I had sat and spoken with a corpse. Or at least that was how it seemed. Mariam was on the verge of death. Certain death.

We were determined to get some medical help for her the next morning, though it seemed doubtful that she would make it. I walked slowly past the other huts in the kraal and made my way up the dark pathway. My knees were weak, and I was nauseated. As I reached the top of the small hill, my vision blurred as tears of pity and helplessness welled up in my eyes.

I will come back to the story of Mariam, but first let me share some facts about AIDS, this curse that has been put on the people of Africa. I must confess that I cannot claim to have the cold, professional objectivity most often given to this kind of discussion. What I have seen and what I have learned about AIDS repulses me at many levels, and all I hope to achieve in this discourse is to add my voice of protest against the deliberate destruction of the remaining strands of African dignity.

What the Experts Say

According to most experts, AIDS has overtaken malaria as the leading cause of death in Africa. The United Nations, in a 1998 report, stated that the AIDS epidemic was responsible for one out of five deaths in Africa.[13] The consensus is that the spread of AIDS and its impact on

Africa has far exceeded what is being experienced in other parts of the world. In Africa, AIDS is affecting all segments of the population, not just special-risk groups as is the case, for example, in America.

Peter Piot, executive director of UNAIDS, the organization responsible for coordinating the fight against AIDS, says that AIDS is the most formidable challenge ever faced by modern medicine, with the potential to undermine the massive improvements made this century in global health and well-being.

Even if we were to find a cure for HIV (human immunodeficiency virus) today, millions of people are already living with the infection, meaning that the burden of AIDS will continue to be severely felt. "This is only the tip of the iceberg," Piot said.[14]

As a non-scientific person, I initially accepted with sadness the prevailing prognosis that Africa as a continent is terminally ill and that it is just a matter of time before she finally gives up the ghost. I was helpless in my observation. The continent has endured many hardships, I mused, but this time it really looked like the end of the road. Or was it?

What really is this thing called AIDS anyway? Where did it come from? And why is it unleashing its venom so ferociously on Africa and not on the rest of the world?

The weight of these questions struck me one evening as I strolled alone through a park in the city of Durban in South Africa. I was a stranger in the town, but I remember trying my best to melt into the surroundings and not attract any undue attention to myself. I had been warned about walking alone at night, and so it was against my own good sense that I decided to go to the park as the dusk of evening ushered in the end of another scorching day under the African sun.

Taking my perch on an empty bench in the middle of the park, I was taken in by the number of couples coiled up in the grass or simply sitting romantically in the evening shadows. I looked around in wonder at the power of sex and its ability to blind mankind. The acts of intimacy and fondling that were going on obtrusively around me made me both uncomfortable and curious, and I couldn't help wondering how many of the young men and women in the park that Saturday evening would succumb to the dreaded virus.

As I sat there ruminating, a young man of about thirty walked over and sat down on the bench next to me. I remained stoic and displayed no visible interest in him despite the distraction that his presence created. After a few minutes, I stole a glance in his direction, and in that brief moment, I saw in the young man's face the other side of the story. The expression on his face was one of total resignation to the worst that life can offer. The young man looked lonely, lost, and defeated.

We never spoke. We didn't even so much as acknowledge the existence of each other. But in the deep silence that separated us, I tried to imagine what that young man might be thinking in light of the drama that was being played out in the dark shadows of that park. And I remembered an old R&B song whose lyrics suddenly found some meaning. The song was about a guy who had no money, no job, no place to call his own—only one thing he could guarantee to his lovely lady: "I can still make love to you." The connection struck me at first as humorous, but then it triggered some serious questions about the role of sex in the seemingly endless erosion of the quality of life in Africa.

There is no doubt that sex, with its alluring and deceptive qualities, is one of the most powerful forces that confront mankind. The urge for sexual intercourse, especially among men, is instinctive, insatiable, and often blinding. It is a commodity with an ever-present market, a force that no law can bridle, and an illusion that possesses and subdues both the great and the small. Sex knows no boundaries. It is found in books, in the movies, on the billboards, and even in the clothes we wear. Most of all, it is in the minds of people.

The preoccupation with sex, as far as I know, has been with mankind since the beginning of time. It is the one thing over which neither Jew nor Gentile, American nor Zulu can claim to have a monopoly. In this one realm there is no distinction between rich and poor, white and black.

So therein lay my first question: If AIDS is transmitted sexually, why is it that there is such an epidemic in Africa and not in other parts of the world? Suddenly the story behind the AIDS epidemic in Africa did not make any sense. Given the widespread sexual immorality in Europe, the United States, and other so-called developed countries, the logic would be that AIDS should have also become widespread in those populations.

Instead, almost two decades after it was first identified and described in medical literature, AIDS in the United States and Europe has remained rigidly confined to special-risk groups: homosexuals, drug users, and transfusion patients. Of the 70,000 Americans diagnosed each year with AIDS, at least ninety percent are drug users.[15] Yet the Western scientific community has convinced the world that AIDS is African in origin and primarily an African problem. Many leading scientists in this field have gone out of their way to argue that AIDS originated in some remote place in central Africa with some "lost tribe" in whom the virus had been present for centuries. According to this now widely accepted theory, Africans acquired the infection from monkeys.

Like many Africans, I was initially offended by these theories. But I objected not so much because of their underlying racial interpretations but because they diverted attention away from what I believe to be the core issue in the purported spread of AIDS in Africa.

The important question is: Does it really matter where AIDS started? My answer is yes, it most certainly matters. Anyone who has ever had the experience of getting on a wrong train will agree that getting on the right train is the only way you can be assured of reaching your destination. Once the train begins its journey, there is little that one can do but be carried along by the momentum. So, if the assumptions about the source and nature of the African AIDS epidemic are incorrect, it stands to reason that what is being done to contain and eliminate it is also incorrect.

Let me rephrase the question: Is it possible that the scientific community is applying inappropriate and ineffectual strategies for for containment and control of AIDS because of wrong assumptions? An honest answer to this question would have to be, yes, it is possible. Why? Because people can make mistakes. It's that simple. Scientists have been known to blame some non-infectious diseases on infectious microbes only to find out millions of dollars later that they were wrong. Let me give you an example.

Hidden in foreign-language materials and the footnotes of obscure sources lies the story of SMON (subacute myelo-optico neuropathy), a frightening disease epidemic that struck Japan while the war on polio was accelerating in the 1950s. In many ways, SMON anticipated the later AIDS epidemic. For fifteen years, the Japanese science establishment mismanaged the SMON syndrome, where virtually all research efforts were guided by the assumption, later proved wrong, that the disease was caused by a virus. Ignoring strong evidence to the contrary, researchers continued to assume that SMON was contagious and scrutinized one virus after another in search of the infectious agent.

Year after year the epidemic grew, despite public health measures to prevent the spread of infection. In the end, medical doctors were forced to admit that their misdiagnosis of the disease had actually been responsible for the spread of SMON. Once the truth about SMON could no longer be ignored, the episode culminated in lawsuits filed by the thousands of remaining victims.[16]

AIDS: The Untold Story

Let's get back to the AIDS story. The idea that AIDS is the result of a deadly virus infection called HIV was first propounded at an international press conference in the United States in April 1984 and adopted almost immediately worldwide.

The theory seemed to be validated scientifically when Dr. Robert Gallo of the National Institute of Health (U. S.) published four long papers in a single issue of the journal *Science* purporting to have identified the HIV virus as the primary cause of AIDS and to have produced a diagnostic test for it.

The theory became the basis of an industry that has since received tens of billions of dollars for research and treatment in Europe and North America, with more than $45 billion contributed by American taxpayers alone. Gallo's apparent discovery was hailed as adding "another miracle to the long honor roll of American medicine and science," although it was to herald a worldwide panic over sex, with predictions that millions would die as the virus spread surreptitiously.[17]

Since that time, the AIDS train has been rolling down the HIV track with such momentum that few people have had the guts to stand up and ask if we might actually be on the wrong train. Despite the issue's importance, journal editors and advisers seem to reason that since "everyone" agrees that HIV is the cause of AIDS, anyone seriously proposing otherwise is eccentric and illogical. Dissidents are dangerous, it is argued, because if people doubt HIV's role in AIDS, they might not heed warnings about the need to change sexual habits.[18]

Yet most people who read, hear, and talk about AIDS do not know that after spending billions of dollars, researchers are still, to this day, unable to explain how HIV damages the immune system, and they know even less about how to stop it. More than a decade after the discovery, no vaccine is in sight, and confusion reigns.

I do not want to delve too deeply into this controversy, but I think it is worth pointing out that a growing number of credible scientists are raising their voices against the theory that links HIV to AIDS. Dr. Joseph Sonnabend, a New York physician and founder of the American Foundation for AIDS Research (AmFAR) had this to say about it: "The marketing of HIV, through press releases and statements, as a killer virus causing AIDS, without the need for any other factors, has so distorted research and treatment that it may have caused thousands of people to suffer and die."[19]

What Is Really Ailing Africa?

At virtually every major conference on AIDS, there are endless discussions about ways to care for those who are already HIV-positive and to contain the spread of the disease. The discussions are usually centered on how to change people's sexual behavior to protect those who are yet to be infected, and the need to lobby for cheaper drugs that can turn AIDS from a death sentence into a chronic but survivable medical condition.

Yet, wh ile health experts fixate on HIV, hundreds of thousands of sub-Saharan Africans lack access to safe water, and even more lack proper sanitation. An estimated fifty million preschool children suffer from protein-calorie malnutrition.[20] Because of these and many other basic problems that arise out of poverty, many people in Africa run a high risk of contracting diseases like cholera, tuberculosis, dysentery, and respiratory infection, all of which in fact constitute the primary threats to African lives.

Despite these realities, AIDS experts expect us to accept that something "new" is afoot in Africa and that it is caused by a new agent, HIV. Suddenly, a new disorder, caused by a new agent, has appeared. The old diseases and their deleterious effects on the immune system are no longer operative.[21]

Even more disturbing are the distortions of the AIDS problem in Africa that are built on unverifiable statistics. Most of us read about the percentages of Africans who are either HIV-positive or who are dying of AIDS, but rarely do we question the basis for that information.

President George W. Bush, on June 20, 2002, in a White House Rose Garden announcement, joined in the growing chorus of people making claims about the percentage of Africans suffering from AIDS. "In Africa, the disease clouds the future of entire nations and threatens to hold back hopes of an entire continent," Bush said. "In the hardest-hit countries of sub-Sahara Africa, as much as one-third of the adult population is infected with HIV, and ten percent or more of the schoolteachers will die of AIDS within five years."[22] On what premises are such reports based?

The reality is that in Africa and much of the Third World, HIV tests are simply *not* required for an AIDS diagnosis. In the absence of adequate laboratory facilities in much of Africa, the medical world has been forced to come up with a definition for AIDS in Africa that is different from the one used in developed countries.

In Africa, AIDS is diagnosed according to the World Health Organization's 1986–87 "Bangui" definitions, which can best be described as a laundry list of common nonspecific symptoms, such as cough, fever, diarrhea, tuberculosis (TB), and a cancer called Kaposi's sarcoma. In other words, most patients are classified as AIDS cases without laboratory proof that they have either immunodeficiency or HIV infection. All that is required for a person to be diagnosed as having

AIDS is the presence of certain clinical conditions. The result is that most news reports on AIDS in these regions are based on estimates rather than actual cases or actual deaths, and often what is being counted is nonspecific, as many of these estimates are for "HIV / AIDS."

The claim that millions of Africans are threatened by AIDS makes it politically acceptable to use the continent as a laboratory for vaccine trials and the distribution of toxic drugs of disputed effectiveness, such as AZT. On the other hand, campaigns that advocate monogamy or abstinence, along with ubiquitous media claims that "safe sex" is the only way to avoid AIDS, have the effect of scaring Africans away from visiting public health clinics for fear of receiving a fatal AIDS diagnosis. Even Africans with treatable medical conditions such as tuberculosis but who believe wrongly that they have AIDS fail to seek medical attention because they think that they have an untreatable disease."[23]

My Lucky Cousin

Let me return now to the story of my cousin Mariam—Mariam, the living corpse who was on the verge of certain death from AIDS. The story has both a happy and a sad ending. The happy ending is that Mariam's health improved dramatically after she was provided with simple medical treatment, food supplements, clean blankets, and potable drinking water. Her "miraculous" recovery generated all manner of speculations from those who know her, some of them bordering on the absurd.

The sad ending to the story is that Mariam, like most of the people living in the Randago village, would remain trapped in her world of poverty. In that world, she would not be able to afford the expensive medicines, nutritious food, and clean water that would be needed for her full recovery. She would remain vulnerable to diseases that would keep her perpetually weakened and cripple her capacity to work her way back into being a productive member of the community.

Mariam's remarkable turnaround prompted me to wonder just how many other Africans are dying from causes that have never been properly diagnosed and are simply assumed to be AIDS, but which are really preventable diseases that simply go hand in hand with being poor. The real tragedy is that the appropriate cures for sick people like Mariam have been relegated to the sidelines and now receive little funding or attention due to the unbalanced focus on AIDS. Billions of dollars in biomedical funds—funds that were previously earmarked to fight African poverty and diseases like malaria, tuberculosis, and leprosy—are now being diverted into sex counseling and condom distribution. Thousands of social scientists have shifted their attention from the real problems that continue to ravage Africa, and are now focusing their efforts on behavior-modification programs and AIDS-awareness surveys.

Despite the scholastic arguments that can be made for or against the various theories surrounding the AIDS crisis, one thing is certain: If AIDS were a real threat to the world community as some would claim, we would see a global coalition against the scourge that would rival, if not surpass, the coalition against terrorism. But it is simply not that kind of threat.

So, as time marches on, we continue to conduct more surveys, and we try to measure and derive better estimates of the depth of the human suffering on the African continent. We never seem to be able to get enough information, so we surf the Internet and design better data-collection instruments to get ever-better statistics on the number of dead and dying. Our governments take on more loans to buy condoms and toxic drugs from multinational corporations. We stare blankly at the fingers that point at us and blame us for our own suffering. It must be God's punishment for our immorality, we say. And then we move on silently to the next funeral.

In the meantime, poverty continues to march on, undaunted in its devastation as it continues to ravage the lives of more and more Africans. All around us, we see the fruits of poverty—starvation, ignorance, illiteracy, crime, filth—and slowly we become blinded even to the basic ideals that we once held so high. Yes, this disease—this old disease called poverty—is the real enemy of Africa. And AIDS is just another fruit on that deadly tree.

CHAPTER FIVE

Debt Bondage

Africa's debt burden is the new economy's chains of slavery.

—Jesse Jackson

The date was April 3, 1999. It was my birthday, and I remember wishing that I were somewhere else, celebrating what was supposed to be a milestone in my life. I had spent the previous three weeks traveling through several African countries, visiting projects to which Oikocredit, my employer, had advanced loans.

Oikocredit is a twenty-five-year-old, Netherlands-based institution that provides long-term loans to businesses in the developing world. The institution is funded largely by private investors who are motivated more by principles of social justice than by the desire to realize economic returns on their investments. My role in the organization was to coordinate its lending in Africa.

Although I had been with the institution for almost a year, I was still on a steep learning curve in which I found myself continually amazed at the complexities of doing business on our continent. The trip that I was on had been especially taxing due to the number of problems that

I had encountered with our borrowers. A number of them were in arrears, and some were in serious default.

At about 10:30 in the morning of that fateful day, I arrived at the office of one of our borrowers for my final meeting before returning to the Netherlands. I want to share some elements of my conversation with him as an entry point into my discussion of Africa's debt problem. Before doing so, however, I should point out that I have altered a number of details in order to protect the identity of the project.

The borrower was in this case a non-governmental organization (NGO) that had been established some years earlier to provide small loans and other financial services to some eight hundred poor women in the community. According to the loan proposal, which I had finished rereading on the airplane, the eight hundred women were the main stakeholders in the NGO. They had been presented as economically disadvantaged people whose lives the project would endeavor to uplift.

Prior to my arrival at the project site, I had received information from sources close to the NGO that its management had misappropriated the proceeds of the $500,000 (U. S.) loan it had received from Oikocredit. According to this information, the organization was virtually bankrupt, and the likelihood of its ever being able to repay our loan was slim at best.

Upon receiving this information, I was tempted to walk away and not waste time on what appeared to be a lost cause. I considered suggesting to my employer that we simply cut our losses and write off the loan. Yet, even as this thought ran through my mind, I knew very well that walking away without demanding some gesture of accountability or retribution would only send the wrong message to other existing and potential borrowers. It would also allow the guilty parties to get away without having to pay for their actions.

My next impulse was to hit the organization hard with some legal actions that would make it clear to one and all that it did not pay to default on a loan obligation. I considered just how ruthless I should be in order to show the manager, and anybody else who was watching, that we took our business very seriously.

We were, however, faced with a dilemma. To take the tough stance of legally foreclosing on the loan would effectively mean taking the institution down. This was certainly not our desire, and the fallout from that decision would be devastating for the community. I was also fully aware that, as a lender, Oikocredit had virtually no leverage in forcing changes in management. That kind of action was the prerogative of the eight hundred poor, mostly illiterate women stakeholders who probably had no concept of what was going on in the organization. Despite their legal rights and responsibilities as the owners of the organization, the women had been rendered essentially powerless by the cunning and manipulative management team who had not only effectively transformed the organization into a vehicle for attracting donor money for their own benefit, but had gone on to misuse the funds entrusted to them on behalf of the designated beneficiaries.

From a strictly legal perspective, it was the eight hundred women who owed us $500,000. But this was more than just a legal matter. We were faced with a moral issue whose resolution depended on the interpretation that we gave it.

Viewed from a different angle, I couldn't help wondering what led my employer, Oikocredit, to lend so much money to this relatively weak entity? I was later to learn that the period in which the loan had been made to the African project happened to be a period in which Oikocredit was under intense pressure to place more funds in the field. After having gone through some slow years of relatively low liquidity, Oikocredit now found itself awash in a tidal wave of funds as thousands of people in Europe and North America suddenly embraced its vision. Funds poured in, along with directives from these new investors about how the funds should be allocated.

For institutions like Oikocredit, having too much money can be as problematic as not having enough. The pressure to satisfy investor demands can cause project scrutiny to become lax and fuel the temptation to take shortcuts.

To Pay or Not To Pay . . . That Is the Question

The dilemma that I faced with this project and many others like it has brought me to a higher level of appreciation of the dilemma faced not only by many African countries, but also by their lenders. The problem of Africa's debt is a two-sided issue despite the fact that most people view it through narrow lenses that can only distinguish one side, either the lenders or the borrowers, as the exclusively bad guys.

The story of Oikocredit's African project illustrates the twisted relationship between the international financiers and the heavily indebted developing countries. Many of the external debts that now sit heavily on the backs of Africa's poor masses were negotiated by economic managers and political leaders who had little or no intention of ever using the funds as promised to the lenders.

The citizens of these countries were rarely notified or informed of the purpose of the loan or its terms and conditions. The governments often borrowed the funds with the promise of using them to pay for infrastructure such as roads, public services, and health clinics, and to run government ministries. In most cases, they used the loans for projects that did not meet minimum standards of social, ecological, or even economic viability. At times, these loans were used merely to enrich a small group of people or were transferred out of the country to the private bank accounts of government officials.

When examining Africa's debt problem from the angle of misuse and corruption, the lending institutions tend to come out looking like the good guys, who extended their resources in the interest of helping the poor and who have been swindled by the few bad guys. To some extent this perspective has merit, but there is another side to this complex story, the side of lenders who knowingly pumped money into these poor economies for reasons that were anything but compassionate. The World Bank, the IMF, and other bilateral and multilateral lenders have made an enormous contribution to Africa's fiscal mess, and there is no way that they can escape the glare of the spotlight of responsibility.

When the problem became a Crisis

If we are to fully understand Africa's current debt problem, we have to put it in the context of the circumstances that led the lenders to pump so much money into these seemingly weak nations. This story runs almost parallel to the Oikocredit illustration.

Economists are not united on what actually brought on the current global debt crisis, but there are some events that certainly contributed greatly to it. One notable event is the 1973 decision by the members of the Organization of Petroleum Exporting Countries (OPEC) to quadruple the price of oil.

Perhaps the most significant outcome of the decision was that the OPEC countries suddenly found themselves with excess funds for which they had to find safe investments. As it turned out, they simply deposited the funds in commercial banks. The banks, in turn, had to find new places to invest the money.

In the ensuing years, the international banks would go on a lending spree resulting in billions of dollars in loans to developing countries. These loans were often made without appropriate evaluation of the loan requests or proper monitoring of how the loans were used. Due to irresponsible practices of creditor as well as debtor governments, much of the money borrowed was spent on programs that did not benefit the poor. The funds were spent on armaments, large-scale development projects, and private projects often benefiting only the government officials and a small elite.

And then, in 1979, just as the world was beginning to come to terms with the effects of the 1973 oil price hike, OPEC threw the world into yet another tailspin by once again raising the price of oil. The increase in fuel prices resulted in sharp increases in costs of goods and services for which many economies were simply not prepared. The combined impact of the rising price of fuel and the resulting high interest rates eventually spilled over into a worldwide recession.

Not surprisingly, developing countries were hurt the most. Africa was particularly devastated. Many of the countries on the continent that had relied heavily on exporting primary products like tea, coffee, cocoa and cotton were crippled by the worldwide collapse in commodity prices. With their export earnings dwindling and with the loans still having to be repaid, the governments began to experience the fallout from the massive loans they had taken. The borrower countries faced a deepening cash-flow crisis in which they could not keep up with either their domestic commitments or their loan repayments. A crisis was in the making.

The international debt problem finally took center stage in 1982 when Mexico announced that it could no longer pay its foreign debt. The announcement by the Mexican government sent shock waves throughout the international financial community as creditors feared that other countries would do the same. Mexico's move was a loud wake-up call that was interpreted by many that the international financial system was on the brink of collapse.

The crisis resulted in a number of measures being taken over the next several years to stabilize the international financial system. In most cases, the approach was to reschedule the loans and thereby postpone having to face the inevitable avalanche of defaults.

The massive restructuring of loans did provide some breathing space for both the lenders and borrowers, but it was only a matter of time before the problem would again rear its head. In 1996, the World Bank, the IMF, and other major creditors finally recognized the seriousness of the crisis by launching the HIPC (Heavily Indebted Poor Countries) Initiative.

The HIPC Initiative was a significant step, because it recognized the impossibility of resolving the crisis just by postponing payments (rescheduling). Some debt, the lenders acknowledged, would have to be cancelled, including debt owed to the multilateral institutions themselves. However, the amount of write-offs proposed by the lenders under the HIPC Initiative did not even come close to meeting African needs for debt cancellation.

The complexities of the HIPC process, and the harsh structural adjustment programs that have accompanied the intervention of international creditors have actually served to worsen the debt crisis and hamper the social and economic development of HIPC countries. Although the HIPC Initiative had been touted as a scheme to ease the debt burden of the world's most heavily indebted poor countries, its real aim was to protect creditors by using formulas designed to extract the maximum possible in debt payments from the world's poorest economies.

The case of Zambia presents a good example of the myth behind the HIPC Initiative. When the board of directors of the IMF decided that Zambia was eligible for relief on its massive external debt repayments, serious flaws were exposed in the existing debt relief framework. With Zambia's qualification to receive relief under the Initiative, the Zambian government would actually end up being required to pay more in annual debt service to creditors than it had previously.[24]

Zambia's situation was not unique. In fact, it is an example that reveals much about the dynamics of Africa's debt crisis and the fundamental flaws in the international response. Zambia's diligence in pursuing World Bank- and IMF-led reforms resulted in an increase in poverty and the weakening of the country's social services. Its debt burden forced the country to strain its resources to the limit in seeking to meet its huge debt service obligations.

The central problem here is that Africa's debt has become so large in comparison to the continent's income that it simply cannot be repaid. The income generated by many of the indebted countries is so low and so volatile that these countries simply cannot keep up with the demands of their creditors. *To pay or not to pay*, that is the big question as well as the dilemma that stands between the borrowers and lenders in this international game of big money, power, and politics.

The Moral Dimensions of the International Debt

From a purely legalistic point of view, the practice of lending and borrowing of money is a legitimate, acceptable exercise. There is nothing inherently wrong with a developing country borrowing money from internal or external sources, as long as key conditions of *justice* are met on the part of the lender and borrower. However, this *contractual* justice must be located within the broader context of *social* justice.

International debt presents a moral challenge whose resolution affects the dignity, rights, and welfare of some of the most vulnerable men, women, and children in the global community. To focus only on the terms of the loan or on the nations or institutions involved, rather than on the conditions under which the loan was contracted, is wrong, because it attempts to isolate the contractual justice from its context. Sub-Saharan African governments transfer to their creditors several times more than they spend on the health of their people, a fact that cannot be disputed or ignored.

One of the fundamental problems, the implications of which are not understood by many, is the unfair power relationship that governs the borrowing of money by poor countries from the richer countries. Let us say, for instance, that I as an individual or the owner of a business was to borrow money from a bank. In that case, my relationship with the bank would be governed by a set of laws that are administered by courts. If I were to find myself overextended and unable to repay my loan, the law provides a solution known as bankruptcy.

This law of bankruptcy provides individuals or businesses with an opportunity to start again with a clean slate. Under this law, banks acknowledge that the debtor cannot fully pay his or her debts and a court is appointed to assess the situation.

As for countries that borrow money, however, there is no such thing as bankruptcy. There is no procedure or arbitrator. At the international level, it is the creditors themselves, not a court, who set the rules and determine the conditions under which the debtor country will be required to pay its debt. It is precisely this uneven relationship that moves the discussion of the debt problem out of the arena of simple economics into a moral one.

The moral dimensions of the international debt problem extend to how the debt was contracted, who was involved in key decisions, which institutions are now primarily responsible for its resolution, and what moral criteria should be used to articulate, structure, and adjudicate this fabric of relationships.[25] The problem here is that when one's creditors are in charge of making such crucial decisions, the indebtedness crosses over into what can only be described as debt bondage.

Democracy as the Key

There are many ways of looking at the debt problem in Africa. One angle that needs to be given greater attention is the lack of involvement and understanding by ordinary Africans of their fundamental democratic rights as citizens of their countries and stakeholders in the shaping of their destinies. The gross misappropriation and mismanagement of Africa's resources by her leaders found a fertile ground in the ignorance of the disenfranchised masses who, already oppressed by poverty and intimidated into subservience by their rulers, took upon their shoulders the unfair burden of debt that today denies them even the possibility of life's basic necessities.

President Yoweri Museveni of Uganda, in his book, *What is Africa's Problem?*, says, "There is no doubt that lack of political education has contributed to Africa's crisis. Because of lack of political education, people cannot confront the problems affecting their lives. Real issues will not be addressed, let alone resolved."[26]

In the absence of a political awareness among the masses of Africans, we should not expect the future to be any different from the past. Corrupt leaders will continue to be corrupt. Outside forces driven by greed will continue to tie up the continent in legal and financial transactions that will continue to bind the continent from any progress. *If there is no accountability, you cannot stop corruption, and if you cannot stop corruption, you cannot have development.* My conclusion then is that development is intrinsically linked to democracy.

The answer to Africa's debt problem does not lie in simply cleaning up the balance sheet through debt forgiveness. The challenge that stands before me as well as before all those who care to help Africa out of its quagmire is to find the means of empowering ordinary Africans to take responsibility for their future. It is in the sphere of the mind that I believe the battle must begin.

The greater responsibility here lies with the civil society to advocate the rights of the disadvantaged and vulnerable masses who have little knowledge of the world beyond their daily struggles. Contrary to a popular notion, ignorance is *not* bliss. Society must fight ignorance as if it were the plague.

One of the sad outcomes of ignorance is the creation of inward-looking communities that can neither think outside of their narrow existence nor appreciate the value that lies in unity and cooperation with other communities. In the next chapter, we will look at some of the fruits of ignorance: the fragmentation of society and the breakdown in the values that define human worth.

CHAPTER SIX

A House Divided

Every kingdom divided against itself is
brought to desolation, and every city or
house divided against itself will not stand.
—*Jesus Christ*

On Wednesday, January 17, 2001, I woke up to the news that Laurent Kabila, the president of the Democratic Republic of Congo (DRC), was dead. The timing of Kabila's death struck me as ominous, because it just so happened that that was the morning on which I had planned to begin writing this chapter on the crippling effects of Africa's fragmentation. The news caused me to pause and reflect at a much deeper level on the enormous losses that Africa had incurred as a result of conflict.

The DRC conflict, particularly, had been at the forefront of my mind because of some staggering statistics that I had stumbled onto just a few days earlier. According to a study carried out by the International Rescue Committee, an estimated 1.7 million Congolese had died of war-related causes in 1999 and 2000 alone. The *Washington Post* estimated the figures to be even higher, at about three million. [27]

I don't know what to do when I come across statistics like these. My mind freezes, and I am tempted to turn my back and throw my hands in the air when I even begin to consider what this could mean for Africa's future. If these estimates are accurate—or even half-accurate—they suggest a death rate in Congo Kinshasa that surpasses that of any war in recent memory.

The story of the DRC is extremely complex. To fully grasp the social, political, and historical dynamics that have helped to shape it would go way beyond the scope of this book. Nonetheless, it is a story that cannot be brushed aside easily. Given the strategic significance of the country, which I will discuss below, I have decided to use the DRC story as our window into Africa's endless struggle with itself. In this one story, we see some of the historical and contemporary issues that have contributed to both the structuring and fragmenting of many African societies.

What Is So Important about the Congo?

Perhaps the best starting point in reviewing the troubled history of the Democratic Republic of Congo and its serious implications for Africa as a whole is to ask the question: What is so important about the Congo? The answer is both simple and complex. The main reasons for the Congo's strategic importance are its geographical location and size. The country shares borders with nine other states in Africa. A vast territory of 2,345,406 square kilometers, the Congo is nearly twice the size of South Africa, three times the size of Nigeria, five times the size of France, and over eighty times the size of Belgium, its former colonial ruler. As the third largest country on the continent, the Congo spans two time zones. A jet aircraft takes more than two hours to fly over it in any direction.

Economically, the Congo has enormous wealth in natural resources, and therein lies the deeper significance of the present crisis. Known primarily as a minerals-producing economy, the country has such an ecological diversity that it is also rich in non-mineral resources.

Approximately one third of the total area is tropical rainforest. But the total area is dominated by the Congo River Basin, and includes seven great and medium-sized lakes, plus hundreds of rivers and small lakes. Lake Tanganyika, which the country shares with Burundi and Tanzania, is the fifth largest lake in the world. As for the Congo River itself, which gave the country its name, it is one of the five longest rivers in the world and the first in terms of hydroelectric potential.

Part of this potential has already been harnessed through Inga Dam to provide electricity to the Congo and some neighbors, including Zambia and Zimbabwe in southern Africa. *This hydroelectric complex has the potential of lighting up the whole continent of Africa, from Cairo to Cape Town.* With twelve months of rainfall in much of the rainforest and plenty of rain in the two savanna zones on either side of the equator, *the Congo can also feed the entire continent.* It is therefore not difficult to understand why there is so much international interest in what happens in and to the DRC.[28]

The Troubled History of the DRC

The history of the DRC tells a lot, if not the whole story, about the baggage of the past that continues to weigh down so much of the African continent. It is indeed a tragic story of conflict—a long-running, confusing conflict that has seen one of the richest countries in the world degenerate into a basket case of human tragedy.

For most of its history, the Congo was a blank on the map, luring in the greedy and unwary. It was first pillaged by slave kingdoms and foreign slavers, then by predators looking for ivory, rubber, timber, copper, gold, and diamonds. King Leopold of Belgium grabbed it in 1885 and invested a considerable amount of his own fortune to set up what was essentially a private kingdom. His agents forced the inhabitants of the Congo to extract its extraordinary wealth by cutting off hands and executing those who resisted. They set up a brutal, exploitative regime for the extraction of rubber in the interior forest regions of the so-called Free State. Impoverishment and famine followed, and in the process, hundreds of thousands of Africans died.[29]

By the mid-1890s the Congo Basin and its products became a source of great wealth to Leopold, who used his riches to beautify his Belgian capital, Brussels. I can imagine that Brussels would have been a very different city without its Congo connection. There is still today a Congo flavor in the music and food, and Congo exiles can be found plotting in Brussels's bars and hotels, some still referring to their homeland by its former name, Zaire.

But it is the wealth that Belgium extracted from colonial Africa that changed the face of the modern-day capital. Two of Brussels's most elegant thoroughfares, Avenue Louise and Avenue Terveuren, were laid out with money raised from Belgium's adventures in the Congo Basin, and many of the city's most grandiose buildings were funded from the proceeds of rubber, timber, and ivory.[30]

After Leopold came Belgian state rulers. They built some roads and brought in health and education programs, but blocked any political development. When the Congo was finally pitched into independence in 1960, there was total chaos.[31]

By the late 1950s—the threshold of Belgian political withdrawal— about one percent of the inhabitants of the Belgian Congo were of non-African origin and loyalty. But 95 percent of the total assets, 82 percent of the largest units of production, and 88 percent of private savings belonged to foreigners. Here then was a society in which a small group of whites and a very few large overseas firms controlled almost the entire modern economy. [32]

In essence, the Belgians left a country that had not only been plundered, but was ill equipped to govern itself. Within days of independence, the Congo was threatening to split apart. Then out of the chaos came Mobutu Sese Seko, the man who would dominate the country for three decades.

Mobutu came to power with military backing—and succeeded in staying there by successfully playing off one rival army faction against another. Recruited by the CIA in the late 1950s when his country was still a Belgian colony, Mobutu helped to overthrow Patrice Lumumba, the Congo's first and only democratically elected prime minister. Thousands of Congolese lost their lives in the bitter five-year civil war that followed. In 1965, Mobutu, with CIA help, seized power in a coup and changed the name of the country to Zaire.

The one thing for which Mobutu will be remembered was his wild, almost demonic pursuit of wealth at the expense of the welfare of his people and nation. Perfecting a system of rule by theft (called kleptocracy), Mobutu pillaged the public sector, harassing or jailing those who objected. He and his cronies siphoned off hundreds of millions of dollars of the country's mineral export revenues, foreign aid and loans, and private investment.

The effects have been catastrophic. Despite vast mineral wealth (diamonds, cobalt, copper), oil deposits, and immense hydroelectric and agricultural potential, Zaire's per capita income has dropped almost two-thirds since independence in 1960 and is listed as the lowest of all the countries in the world.[33]

Mobutu's impact on people's daily lives was devastating. Extensive corruption crippled public services, including road repair and hospital and school administration. Workers, their salaries stolen, were forced into the system of corruption just to survive.

As Mobutu squandered the profits from much of the country's economic output in European banks and stashed them in European banks, Zaire became the most notorious example of a country where state institutions came to be little more than a way of delivering money to the ruling elite. But the politics of the Cold War ensured Western backing, with the United States using Zaire as a springboard for its operations in neighboring Angola, namely, its support of Unita rebels against the Soviet-backed government.

Ironically, it would take the ethnic conflicts within another country—Rwanda, in this case—to bring an end to the Mobutu regime. In 1994, more than 800,000 people were put to death in the most unambiguous case of state-sponsored genocide since the Nazi extermination of the Jews of Europe.

Kabila's War

After perpetrating the genocide, the Rwandan army and the gangs of killers fled into Zaire where, for reasons not relevant to the focus here, Mobutu gave them shelter and weapons. Two years later, in 1996, the new Tutsi-dominated Rwandan army crossed back over the border and attacked the Hutu camps, intending to set up a buffer zone to protect its western border. The attack worked better than anticipated and the Rwandans, Ugandans, and their Zairian allies kept walking westward until they took the Zairian capital, Kinshasa. Mortally ill, Mobutu fled and Laurent Kabila was installed as president.

One of the first things that Kabila did after becoming president was to change the country's name from Zaire to the Democratic Republic of Congo. Shortly thereafter, Kabila tried to break away from the control of the Rwandans and Ugandans who had helped him to power. He allied himself with their enemies, the Hutu militias in eastern Congo. In an angry response to this move, Uganda and Rwanda jointly launched another rebellion, this time to try to dislodge Kabila. The rebels marched on Kinshasa but met with serious opposition from armed civilians.

Kabila appealed for help from fellow member countries of the Southern African Development Community. He claimed that the Congo was the victim of foreign aggression. Zimbabwe and Namibia responded by sending troops to secure the airport in Kinshasa. The Angolans, who have the strongest and most experienced army in central Africa, sent armored and airborne forces that routed the Rwandans and Ugandans near Kinshasa and stopped their invaders in the east.

The war took many twists and turns, and in July 2000, a peace agreement was signed in Lusaka, Zambia, by the government of the Congo, the three rebel groups, and the five intervening nations. The peace agreement provided a timetable for a ceasefire, the deployment of African military observers supported by UN monitors, the disarming of the militia gangs that roamed eastern Congo, and the eventual withdrawal of all foreign forces.

Not surprisingly, the peace accord did not work. The exploitation of the country by the intervening armies only reinforced the imperialist nature of the invasion. Once in the Congo, the interveners found commercial reasons to stay. The war created huge business opportunities that obscured its primary, political cause. Hundreds of unscrupulous businessmen, mercenaries, arms dealers, and security companies came to the region. Diamonds were the big prize and the main source of foreign exchange for Laurent Kabila.

The tragedy of the Congo is that it is so rich, and yet so weak. Because of this dichotomy, outsiders have always been tempted to interfere. The Congolese have never been allowed to come together, agree on a constitution or elect a government, yet they remain stubbornly nationalistic in a state that disappeared in all but name decades ago.

Despite the relative calm that followed the installation of Laurent Kabila's son, Joseph, as the DRC's new president, the prospects are high that the instability in the country will rumble on for years, if not decades. If there is a message in the violent nature of the death of Laurent Kabila, it is perhaps borrowed from the old adage that those who live by the gun will surely die by the gun.

The Chains of Our History

I have given you a highly abridged version of the history of the Congo crisis. Obviously, there is much more to this conflict, with its web of political, social, and economic complexities, than can be covered in these few pages. But as I said earlier, my primary purpose in telling the story was to use it as a springboard for examining the roots of the conflicts that plague Africa today, and how those conflicts are shaping the continent.

Having now told the tragic story of the DRC, I cannot help but wonder if anything more needs to be said. Yet, no matter how overwhelming the story may be or how potentially destructive its implications appear to be to the entire region's stability, we must remember that the DRC is only one out of fifty-one African countries. Each of these countries has its own complicated history, and each one faces as many of the same explosive social, economic, and political frustrations within its borders as do the people of the DRC.

At the end of 2000, nearly a third of Africa's countries were embroiled in international or civil wars. According to the U. S. Committee for Refugees, more than three million people in fifteen African countries were forced to flee their homes in 1999 because of war, insurgencies, and repression, driving up the number of uprooted people on the African continent to 13.7 million. At least 1.5 million more were uprooted in 2000.[34]

Like the DRC story, most of these contemporary conflicts have their roots in the long stretch of history that encompasses both the slave trade and the colonization of the continent.

For those regions of the continent affected by the slave trade, the continent not only lost a large proportion of its young and able-bodied population, but the people were stripped of their confidence, their culture, and even their ability to develop. Estimates of the total human loss to Africa over the period of the transatlantic slave trade range from 30 million to 200 million. What we cannot even begin to estimate is the psychological damage.

The slave trade engendered in the people an anxiety caused by perpetual fear of being captured and herded away like common animals to a place of no return. The rampant kidnappings of Africans for shipment abroad destroyed community life and fueled hostility and suspicion between communities. As a direct outcome, the social and cultural developments of many African societies were severely retarded.[35]

Underlying the drive to dominate life on the continent were, of course, the forces of economic and political self-interest. In order to meet their economic and administrative needs, colonial powers built some infrastructure, such as railways to carry export commodities, and they educated a few Africans to help them run the colonies. But nowhere in Africa were positive contributions made of any substance.

Countries like Nigeria, Ghana, Kenya, and Zimbabwe were left with only a few rail lines, a rudimentary infrastructure, and a few thousand graduates. Still, they were better off than others. The colonies under Portugal, for instance, were left with even less. When Mozambique became independent in 1975, it had only three dozen college graduates.[36]

Along with extracting material and human resources from Africa, the Western countries left behind insurmountable social, spiritual, political, and economic structures that continue to cripple Africa. The haphazard way in which colonial mapmakers carved up the continent, for instance, has had a tremendous impact on how the social and political landscape of the continent is currently defined. Totally disparate peoples, tribes with less in common than, say, the Dutch and the Italians, were simply thrown together in arbitrary political entities and told to choose governments.

The lack of cultural and linguistic affinity within the newly created nation-states prevented any real national consensus from emerging in most of them. It should come as a surprise to no one that tribalism quickly became the primary expression of identity as well as the driving force in politics throughout the continent.

The removal of communities from their land, governing structures, and way of life forced Africans to adapt new, often Western economic and political models. The groupings of people from different ethnic communities, all fighting for the same already-depleted resources, would later provoke conflict—leading to genocide (Rwanda) and political instability (Zimbabwe, Sierra Leone, Sudan, and Liberia).

To maintain political power, the colonialists pitted different groups against each other by providing "necessary" provisions, such as weapons and medical services. In time, this situation worsened as the post-independent structures duplicated colonial structures and created a breeding ground for corruption and ethnically based political and economic alliances.[37] Without a doubt, by the early 1960s, when most African countries were being granted independence from colonial rule, the continent was, for all practical purposes, already badly crippled.

Valuable Lessons

It is difficult to imagine that we could find anything positive in this horrible chapter of our continent's history. Yet in every tragedy there are lessons that can be used for the journey onward. Africa should have learned some important lessons from the tragic events of her history, but these lessons have been all but lost, resulting in widespread suffering across the continent that makes slavery pale in comparison.

What are these lessons? First, although the slave trade is often portrayed as a frenzy of white people running around the continent capturing black people, we have to recognize that, as with any other trade, it was a business with a well-established chain of suppliers, middlemen, transporters, and buyers, all involved in negotiated contractual dealings. There is no doubt that the European slave buyers made the greater profit from the despicable trade, but we cannot deny that their African partners also prospered greatly from it.

At the initial stage of the trade, parties of Europeans captured Africans in raids on communities in the coastal areas, but this practice soon gave way to buying slaves from African rulers and traders. The inter-communal wars that were waged to procure slaves were intensely destructive. Tens of thousands of Africans were slaughtered by their fellow Africans in the process. The result is that many Africans grew strong and fat on profits made from selling their own people.

Looking at the slave trade from the angle of our own participation is obviously not a popular notion among most of us, but it is one that needs to be highlighted again and again to dispel the notion that the Devil resides only in the West. The argument is so often about *who* is right or wrong, or *who* were the good guys versus the bad guys, when in fact we should be focusing on *what* is right and wrong.

Let me develop this argument a bit further. One of the most unsettling truths about the slave trade is that it was founded on the perception that an African's life was of lesser value than that of a white person. From the perspective of the white traders who bought black people for the price of adulterated brandy and packed them onto slave ships like cattle, it is not difficult to see why they might have considered themselves superior to black people. As the years passed, Europeans became more and more scornful of black people. By the nineteenth century, various theories of black inferiority were developed and exploited to justify the colonization of Africa.

A sad outcome of that experience is that we Africans also came to believe ourselves inferior to white people. Even worse, however, is the evidence that points to our having adopted the same contempt for the lives of our fellow Africans that the white slave traders had displayed. From slavery to oppression to brutal savagery, the history of Africa has moved steadily from what was already evil to atrocities of unthinkable proportions.

While we are often quick to point our fingers at the inhumane way in which the Europeans dealt with Africans, we rarely stop to ask ourselves whether we are in fact different in the treatment of our own people. How much value do we, as Africans, really place on the life of another African? From what I have experienced, the answer would appear to be, not very much.

I remember standing on a street corner in Nairobi one morning where I witnessed the gleeful public stoning of a young man who had been accused of stealing a lady's handbag. The young man died, his bloody face smashed and disfigured by the blows of his assailants. The stoning was horrific enough, but what struck me even more was the ease with which the mob moved on from the slaughter, as though they had just finished a meal.

In his book, *Out of America—A Black Man Confronts Africa*, Keith Richburg displays the same revulsions that I have felt on many occasions upon seeing or reading about some of the nasty incidences that give the outside world such a grotesque picture of Africa. Richburg expresses just how terrified he is of Africa:

> I don't want to be from this place. In my darkest heat here on this pitch-black African night, I am quietly celebrating the passage of my ancestor who made it out.... Had my ancestor not made it out of here, I might have ended up there in that crowd, smiling gleefully, while a man with a cleaver cuts off the hands of a thief. Or maybe I would have been one of those bodies, arms and legs bound together, washing over the waterfall in Tanzania. Or maybe my son would have been set ablaze by soldiers. Or I would be limping now from the torture I received in some rancid police cell....Frankly, I want no part of it.[38]

We can choose to talk all day about the African crisis from the perspective of politics or ethnicity, but we cannot deny the fact that life on the continent has become so devalued that we seem to make a mockery of the evil that outsiders committed in the past.

One needs only to look at some of the recent human tragedies instigated by Africans against Africans to see that African conflicts have reached proportions that defy logic. The Rwandan conflict was the quintessence of the evil that resides beneath the surface in all of us. There was a clear, programmed effort by one ethnic group, the Hutus, to eliminate everybody in the Tutsi minority group simply because they were Tutsis. The logic there was simply to kill everybody, to ensure that nobody got away. We will never know the exact number of people who died in that holocaust. Wild estimates range from 500,000 to one million people.

Another African conflict that stands out in its brutality is the Liberian civil war. Refugees from the Liberian countryside reported many acts of horrific cruelty during that country's years of bloody conflict. One report was that the soldiers of Charles Taylor, the country's current president, were seeking out pregnant women and placing bets on the sex of their unborn children. Then they would rip open the women's wombs and tear out the babies to see who was right.

Evidence of cannibalism also began to trickle out. One soldier told Reuters, "We rip the hearts from their living bodies and put them on the fire, then eat them." According to a Liberian human rights organization, cannibalism in Taylor-controlled territory was so widespread that "there is fear of persecution based on one's fitness for consumption." Taylor's own defense minister accused him of taking part in the practice himself.[39]

And then there are the ghastly tales of Sierra Leone's unending internal warfare. This former British colony, founded in the late eighteenth century by freed slaves, was a difficult place even before the birth of the now infamous Revolutionary United Front (RUF). After an initial bout with democracy upon gaining independence in 1961, Sierra Leone, like the Congo, slid into dictatorship and stayed there through the 1970s and '80s—consistently ranking poorly in the world in infant mortality, per capita income, and life expectancy.

In 1991, a group of about one hundred Sierra Leonean guerrillas, constituting the Revolutionary United Front, launched a campaign to take over the country. The RUF—backed by Charles Taylor, the Liberian warlord—quickly established itself as an unusual rebel group. For one thing, it had no discernible political philosophy or agenda. For another, it was almost unimaginably brutal.

Typically, RUF troops would enter a village and round up its children. Girls, some as young as ten years, would be raped. Boys would be forced to execute village elders and sometimes even their own parents, thus cutting themselves off from their past lives as a first step in their absorption into their new rebel "family." Once children were conscripted, their loyalty was maintained through drugs—they were injected with Speed, which numbed their sensitivity to violence and rendered them dependent on their adult suppliers—and a lifestyle or a livelihood of violence. If conscripts tried to escape, RUF leaders amputated their limbs.

The seemingly endless downward spiral of Africa at the behest of selfish despots gnawed at me late one night as I sat in my living room watching television. On the screen was the rapidly unfolding and predictable drama of yet another African story that would evolve into a highly publicized media spectacle: the ugly land invasion in Zimbabwe. I had been following with deepening sadness the story of a national leader unleashing venomous hatred against his country's minority white community for ills that had been done to his people. From an emotional standpoint, I as an African could feel and even empathize with President Robert Mugabe's anger, even as the rest of the world sneered and poured insults at him for his dastardly actions.

My empathy found further grounding when I saw the unrepentant attitudes of the besieged white farmers—the wealthy minority whose riches were built from the sweat and misery of black Zimbabweans. I identified with the millions of young Africans who were born in a cage of poverty, who lived in squalor while the sneering white minority languished in the splendor of land that their ancestors stole from black people.

But that is where my empathy stopped. As much as I could comprehend the causes of the emotions that were being stirred up by the Zimbabwean politicians, my spirit refused to find reconciliation with the acts of revenge as the solution for the people of that country. I could clearly see that the course of hatred chosen by the Zimbabwean leadership would have the effect of unleashing an even more evil spirit than that which had led the Europeans to plunder Africa.

Whether it is in Zimbabwe, Sierra Leone or the Sudan, the spirit of revenge is a cancer that feeds on itself and ends only when one of the opposing sides is destroyed. This endless cycle of madness that has gripped so many pockets of the continent threatens to keep Africa in an unstoppable spin of human suffering.

Divided We Fall

I would have liked to conclude this chapter with a simple, encapsulating statement about what should be done to ease the burden of conflict in Africa. But I dare not even try. If Africa's problems were the problems of one country and not a continent, they might be more easily addressed. But Africa is not just one country, and we cannot even come close to understanding all the social, political, economic, environmental, and spiritual dynamics that contribute to the instability of the continent. Africans are wonderfully and fearfully complex people. Contrary to many widely held misconceptions about us, we do not have a common traditional culture. We do not have a common language, a common religion, or a common conceptual vocabulary. As a matter of fact, we do not even belong to a common race.

When the outside world looks at me, they see an African—a black African, or a sub-Saharan African. But to those who are close enough to understand me in the context of my society, they can only marvel at the thin line that lies between the beauty and richness of our cultural diversity and the volatility of our nature brought on by the unsettling strife that characterizes our lives.

Sometimes I wish I had the power to raise up my hands and tell the storms of conflict to cease and be still. But I know that only God wields such power. What I do have within my control, however, is my mind. I may not be able to change how other people perceive me, but I can certainly choose how to think. In my own little corner of this complex puzzle of humanity, I can choose to reach out and embrace those things that will bring me into unity with others and reject those things that bring me into conflict.

United, we have a chance to stand and face together the many problems that hinder our progress. Divided, we remain down, forever grovelling, forever fallen.

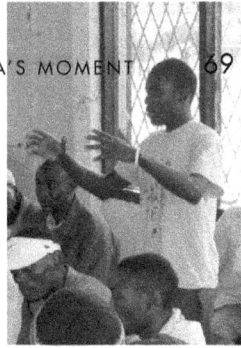

CHAPTER SEVEN

Structural Injustice

*If development is about people, who are both individu-
als and members of a society, there is consequently an
organic link between genuine development and
democracy. In the longer run, neither is sustainable
without the other.*

—*Mwalimu Julius K. Nyerere*

One cold, rainy Monday morning sometime back in 1994, I arrived
at the office of my small consulting practice to learn that Fred, a
young man who had worked under my employ for a couple of years,
had been taken ill and had gone to see a doctor.

My small firm did not have a health care plan for its few staff
members, and as is the case with many developing countries, Kenya
did not have an adequate national health system on which people like
Fred could readily depend for their medical needs. As his employer,
however, I knew that I was morally responsible to help him and the
other staff in whatever way I could.

Fred came to my office after the visit to the doctor and explained
that he needed some money to purchase what I thought were very

expensive drugs. "What did the doctor say was your problem?" I asked him, a bit surprised at the amount of money that he was requesting.

Fred was an honest but rather simple young man, and he looked at me blankly and replied that he had actually not learned the cause of his ailment. He explained that the doctor had examined him for only a few minutes and that he then prescribed three different medicines. As the story unfolded, I came to understand that the doctor had instructed Fred to purchase the drugs from a pharmacy at the front of the private clinic—which just so happened to belong to that same doctor.

"What are these medicines supposed to do for you?" I asked a bit cynically. Fred's answer came as no surprise to me. He did not have the slightest idea. In his ignorance, Fred had essentially entrusted the doctor with his life, and he had accepted the doctor's instructions without question. After all, who was he to question a doctor? Surely the doctor knew what he was doing, didn't he?

Fred's story, like many similar stories that I have encountered along the way, makes me sad whenever I think about it. It is a story of exploitation at its worst: the taking advantage of the helpless whose vulnerability is marked not only by a negative sense of inferiority, but also by a blind trust in the exploiter. It is a story to which Africa needs to pay heed, for it is, in fact, the story of Africa and its frustrated journey toward our so-called development.

The Road to Structural Adjustment

Over the years, the forces of "development" have espoused and discarded many theories and approaches to developing the underdeveloped. In the early 1960s, when most African countries were undergoing their transitions from colonialism, strong emphasis was placed on education. During that period, large amounts of foreign aid funds were channeled into the construction of new schools, along with teacher training and scholarship programs.

Not long after that, the thinking changed, and agriculture became the perceived key to developing the Third World. The underlying argument was that if eighty percent of Africans live in the rural areas, then foreign investments must be directed toward the countries' agricultural sectors. Massive amounts of funds were allocated to large-scale, mostly government-run farming projects. That concept, too, ran its course before boredom set in and a new theory gained acceptance.

The development fads have been many. From basic needs (health care, food, and housing) to infrastructure to industrialization, the tide has shifted again and again, with politics generally being the driving motivation. For the most part, little of substance was achieved in any of these phases. Of all the fads, however, none have been more damaging to Africa than the structural adjustment programs (SAPs) that were imposed on the developing countries by the World Bank and the IMF in the early 1980s.

Broadly speaking, structural adjustment represents a developmental theory that has been promoted by the West as an honest attempt at integrating "developing" countries into the world trading system in order to help accelerate their growth and development. In substance, the theory required that the developing countries:

- prune their government bureaucracies
- remove government involvement from economic activities
- cut government expenditures, especially on social services and subsidies
- introduce user fees in education and health care
- raise food prices
- cut or contain wages
- privatize state-owned enterprises
- devalue their currency
- eliminate or reduce protection for the domestic market
- reduce restrictions on the operations of foreign investors

Underlying these demands was the basic assumption that the adoption of these "open market" policies would somehow catapult the poor countries into the global arena. Unfortunately, what many people did not stop to ask is: If eighty percent of Africans are poor, barely literate peasants with no capital and virtually no links to the modern, industrial economy, then how in the world do we expect them to be integrated into the global marketplace simply by changing our macroeconomic policies?

It doesn't take a genius to see just how flawed this concept was as an instrument of development. The misconception was that human progress could somehow be achieved by focusing on policies, structures and institutions, and not on the people themselves. In other words, it didn't matter how poor, hungry, or uneducated the people were. The markets, it was assumed, would somehow take care of the disparities and lift the underlings to prosperity.

Market conditionalities were imposed on these poorer economies despite the fact that they had inadequate formal markets, almost no external markets, and few industries or even processing facilities for their primary products. Most of the African countries that accepted these conditions lacked sufficient infrastructure, including roads, warehouses, and telecommunications. Like Fred, we humbly accepted the new medicine without so much as stopping to ask ourselves for whose benefit the prescriptions were written in the first place.

Underlying the introduction of the structural adjustment programs was also the misleading perception that progress can be measured in terms of movements in the gross domestic product (GDP). In simple terms, the GDP is the measure of wealth that has been created in a country during a specific period, usually a year. The GDP says nothing about who created that wealth, how it was created, or how it was distributed among the people of that country. The narrow-minded view of measuring human worth in monetary terms has been perhaps the greatest influence on contemporary economic thinking.

The advocates of the growth philosophy have maintained that economic growth is the key to ending poverty, stabilizing the population, protecting the environment, and achieving social harmony. Yet during this same period, the number of people living in absolute poverty has continued to rise. In addition, indicators of social and environmental disintegration have risen sharply nearly everywhere.[40]

Although economic growth did not necessarily create these problems, it certainly has not solved them. The countries who have implemented these economic growth programs have not only suffered the loss of subsidies for social services and the burden of heavy debt, but they have also fallen victim to tariff liberalization and the reckless implementation of other open-market policies that have only served to hold the door open for multinational corporations.

In recent years, multinational corporations have emerged as the dominant governance institutions on the planet, with the largest among them reaching into virtually every country of the world and exceeding most governments in size and power. Increasingly, it is the corporate interest, more than the human interest, which defines the policy agendas of states and international bodies, although this reality with its implications has gone largely unnoticed and un-addressed.[41]

Dependency and Exploitation

After almost three decades of the Western world pushing the drug of development to the Third World, the countries of Africa, like many of their counterparts in Asia and Latin America, have become helplessly addicted. Walter Rodney, in his classic book, *How Europe Underdeveloped Africa*, uses the analogy of a young animal suckling its mother to illustrate the helpless dependency that has resulted in Africa being assigned to the heap of eternal underdevelopment:

> When a child or the young of any animal species ceases to be dependent upon its mother for food and protection, it can be said to have developed in the direction of maturity. Dependent nations can never be considered developed.... A formerly colonized nation has no hope of developing until it breaks effectively with the vicious circle of dependence and exploitation.[42]

Dependency and exploitation are the two words that come to mind when I look at my own country, Kenya, and I see the effects of the power and control of our "developers" over the lives of our people. In 1997, Kenya experienced the shock treatment that the IMF metes out to countries that do not operate as the IMF requires. At a time of severe economic hardship, the IMF decided to shut off the taps on which Kenya had become almost hopelessly dependent.

As is the case whenever the IMF pulls the plug on a country, the IMF's actions in Kenya triggered a spate of capital flight, followed by a surge in interest rates, inflation, and an economic depression that would push the country to the brink of collapse. Like a helpless baby suddenly plucked from its mother's breast, Kenya went into a free-fall.

Many local businesses, already suffering under the ill-conceived structural adjustment policies that the IMF had previously forced upon the country, had no choice but to close down. The number of unemployed soared, adding to the masses who already languished below the line of destitution and misery.

By July 2000, the country was facing perhaps the worst economic crisis in its history. To add insult to injury, even the weather seemed to join in the hostility. For the second year running, the seasonal rains failed to come. In some areas people were dying from hunger, and many were permanently impoverished by the loss of their livestock. Electricity and tap water were being rationed, available only for a few hours a day.

To put it simply, Kenya was in a desperate situation that was getting steadily worse. And then, in August 2000, the news broke that the IMF had agreed to resume lending to Kenya. The public response to the news was euphoric. Given the grim circumstances, it is not difficult to see why many people would have viewed the resumption of funding by the IMF as good news.

In its moment of distress, Kenya needed salvation. From a human perspective, there was no way out. It was either the IMF or the deep blue sea. The Kenyan government, with its back against the wall, finally accepted the tough conditions of the IMF.

The following excerpt from an article in *The Economist*, entitled "Dancing in Kenya to the Donors' Tune," speaks for itself:

> The conditions for the new three-year $198m IMF loan are the toughest ever imposed by the Fund on any government. They contain more than sixty separate elements. The loan, which will unlock a further $300m from other donors and lenders, represents a virtual surrender of the country's sovereignty.
>
> The IMF is insisting, for a start, that the Kenyan parliament must debate and pass a new corruption law. That, however, disguises the fact that the details of the law have already been prescribed by the Fund regardless of parliament's deliberations....
>
> The government will have to draw up a daily balance sheet for inspection by IMF officials. As a reward, Kenya will receive $18m immediately to help mitigate the effects of the drought. After that, however, the aid will be delivered in such thin slices that the slightest deviance from the program will mean that it can be stopped instantly.
>
> There will be no leeway. Kenya is being treated so firmly not just because of its own bad record, but to show other African governments that if they too want aid, they must rule their countries in a way the IMF approves of.[43]

If Kenya's economic well-being were dependent on the graces of the donor community in the past, the new deal with the IMF ensured that the country would henceforth be effectively bound to the whims of those who understand life only in financial terms. These purveyors of money would not only gleefully dangle the carrot of money as a reward for complete obedience, but would also use whatever whips they deemed necessary to ensure that their economic interests were served.

David C. Korten, author of *When Corporations Rule the World*, asks whether development efforts would have different results if, instead of being *growth*-centered (with people regarded only as a means of achieving growth), they were *people*-centered—with people being both the purpose and the primary instrument. In answering his own question, he concludes that "the task of people-centered development in its fullest sense must be the creation of life-centered societies in which the economy is but one of the instruments of good living—not the purpose of human existence.[44]

According to the *South Commission Report*, development is "a process which enables human beings to realize their potential, build self-confidence, and lead lives of dignity and fulfillment. It is a process that frees people from the fear of want and exploitation. It is a movement away from political, economic, or social oppression. Through development, political independence acquires its true significance. And it is a process of growth, a movement essentially springing from within the society that is developing."[45]

The message here is that human progress needs to be discussed in terms that transcend economics. We can adopt new policies, build factories and hold lavish conferences on development, but we cannot get around the fact that real development is about people. Without the collective efforts of its people, a nation cannot progress. To participate in this progress, however, people need to be enlightened, empowered, and respected both by their leaders and those from the outside who interact with them.

CHAPTER EIGHT

Breaking the Chains

The moral progression of a people can
scarcely begin till they are independent.
—*James Martineau*

O ne of the stories that have fascinated people for years is the spectacular exodus of the Jews from Egypt. This story has been the inspiration of such blockbuster movies as *The Ten Commandments* and, more recently, the animated musical *The Prince of Egypt*. It is a story of faith, hope, and the complexities of human nature.

The epic begins with a solemn promise from God to Moses, a highly privileged Jew whose life had been miraculously spared as an infant and who had been given opportunities that most Jews of the day could only dream about. Moses had lived a sheltered life as an adopted child in the house of Pharaoh. In spite of the Egyptians' disdain for the Jews, Moses had grown up as the son of Pharaoh's daughter—the grandson of Pharaoh.

Yet throughout all those years, he never forgot his roots. His identity was inextricably tied to that of his people, the Jews, who for nearly four hundred years had suffered untold miseries at the hands of the powerful exploiters, the rich Egyptians whose vast empire had been built on the backs of slaves. Moses must have hated to see the injustice that was being done to the Jews. He must have wished that there was something he could do to change the course of his people's history. In his moments of solitude, he must have anguished in guilt over his own comforts and felt alienated by the wall of inequality that divided him from the Jewish slaves—his people.

Then one day, unable to contain any longer the emotion and bitterness that had been pent up over the years, Moses unleashed his wrath on an unsuspecting Egyptian man who represented, for him, everything that he so disdained about the world into which he had been conscripted. And he held nothing back. It was a moment of unbridled rage at "the system," a burst of self-righteous indignation at a cruel and unjust world. The hapless victim died on the spot.

The news that the adopted grandson of Pharaoh had killed an Egyptian official must have sent shock waves throughout the empire. The tabloids, the networks, and the rumor mills of the day must have gone into overdrive. This was big news. If there was one thing that the Egyptians feared, it was the constant threat of an uprising by the Jewish slaves, and this was the kind of spark that could ignite such a revolution.

We can only speculate as to what Moses had in mind when he killed the Egyptian. We do not know if his intention was to cause the slaves to revolt. The Bible story, recorded in the Book of Exodus, does not tell us. We can imagine, however, that Moses was no fool and that he was fully aware that he was crossing a line over which there would be no turning back. In his privileged position, he had been given the best education that any child could have received, and it enabled him to see the big picture, a perspective which the toiling masses had neither the luxury nor the time to acquire.

My own speculation is that Moses' action was a case of premeditated murder. Moses must have wanted to catalyze the Jews' circumstances by hurting someone or doing something that would cause the establishment to sit up and listen. He must also have been waiting for the day in which he would prove to the Jews that he was not a traitor, that he was not a part of the system of evil that held them in bondage. Maybe his act of aggression would finally bring them to accept him as truly one of their own. Maybe he could even be a hero.

This incident in the life of Moses speaks volumes to me as I consider the options before us Africans, particularly those of us who have had the opportunity to view the panorama of suffering, exploitation, and hopelessness in which so much of Africa is engulfed. As an educated, fairly enlightened African, I have been pushed to the edge of reason by my exasperation with the specter of human depravity against the background of a smiling, well-fed, and progressing Western world. I have experienced a mixture of helplessness and anger at a world that thrives on inequality and uses its power and resources to erect barriers that effectively seal the fate of the poor. I have seen the damaging effects of globalization on the lives of the poor.

In one way, I can relate to Moses. I can empathize with the emotions with which he must have struggled before finally reaching his dramatic breaking point. On the other hand, I can look at what Moses did and shake my head at the naïveté of his approach to a problem that was so much bigger than he. Moses should have known better than that. This one miscalculation would cost him dearly and teach him some lessons that he never would have learned sitting at Pharaoh's knee.

Death to the Enemy

Re-reading the story of Moses' murder of the Egyptian reminded me of another incident in history, one that took place on November 29, 1999. It was the opening day of the World Trade Organization (WTO) conference, and the city of Seattle marked the date by erupting in violence and rioting.

I can recall sitting transfixed in front of the television as I watched the display of anger and frustration by the many activists who took to the streets. The protesters saw the WTO as the symbol of the evil and greed that was destroying life for millions of people around the world.

They argued that the WTO was the ugly face of the rich nations who were shredding the environmental, labor, health, and safety laws to pry open markets for unrestrained exploitation.

The protesters, hundreds of them, fought with riot police who set off tear gas and shot rubber bullets to try to quell the demonstration. In response, the protesters blocked streets, smashed shops, lit bonfires, and eventually even succeeded in forcing the cancellation of the opening ceremony. So bad were the demonstrations that Seattle's mayor declared a state of civil emergency and a dusk-to-dawn curfew, a rare occurrence in America.

Some weeks after the Seattle mayhem, I asked myself just what had been achieved by the millions of dollars of damage in Seattle, or by the lives that had been lost in similar protests elsewhere. Who were the winners and who were the losers? And, perhaps most important of all, were the poor, hungry souls of Africa (or anywhere else for that matter) better off because the McDonald's on Main Street had been burned down? How many of Pharaoh's men would we have to kill, how much of his property would we have to destroy to bring positive change to our miserable lives?

The events of September 11, 2001, the day of the shocking terrorist attacks on the United States, raised the stakes to a level that no one could have anticipated or even imagined. The whole world stopped dead in its tracks and watched in shock as the forces of hatred and anger unleashed a venom of destruction that brought untold pain, suffering and loss, but still failed to change the "system."

As the world began to come to terms with the new realities of insecurity and instability brought about by the terrorist attacks on the United States, and as the warships set off from the United States in search of the elusive enemy, I felt a sadness coming over me that I am sure was felt by millions across the globe. I realized that the tit-for-tat mentality that drives some activists to destroy life or property as a means of bringing about change is not only misguided, but is ultimately more damaging than helpful to the cause of justice.

A New Level of Thought

Moses was a man with a cause, a valid cause that moved him to the edge of himself. Yet the course of action that he chose to take was not only naïve, but it also showed that he had not yet come to the understanding that lasting change is brought about not by violence, but by a transformation in the hearts of people.

We, too, need to understand that the end of poverty and suffering on our continent requires an organic change in how we see ourselves and the world around us. Practical measures alone will not solve the basic problems, which are human attitudes and behavior. Our material poverty, for example, is a manifestation of humanity's spiritual poverty—our hunger for power, our unbridled self-interest above the common good, and our fear that if we share, we will not have enough for ourselves.

Meeting the challenges ahead of us will require that we set ourselves on a new platform of thought, that we have a clear and shared understanding not only of the direction in which we should walk, but of our ultimate destination. Our mandate will be to find unity and solidarity in working together, to honor the dignity of even the most resource-poor, to trust in their innate capabilities, and to love enough to give ourselves in service to them. The reward for our own accomplishments will be greater self-worth and validation of the dignity of all of us.

The time has come for us, the people of Africa, to break the chains of the past and to set our sights on a new world that is beckoning from the horizon. Let us learn from our past, but let us not dwell on it. Let us neither dread nor fear the future, even though it may be no less painful than the past. Let us answer the urgent call for radical change from within ourselves. The first step involves forgiveness and repentance— forgiveness of those who have so willfully trespassed against us, and repentance for our own contributions to Africa's dark history. We may be hard pressed on every side, but we are not crushed; perplexed, but not paralyzed; persecuted, but not abandoned; struck down, but not destroyed. Yes, Africa may be wounded, but thank God she is still alive.

CHAPTER NINE

Looking to the Future

> God said, "Go and build a better world,"
> And I said, "How?
> The world is such a big place,
> And so complicated now,
> And I'm so young and helpless,
> There's so little I can do."
> And God in all His wisdom said,
> "Just build a better you."
>
> —*Author unknown*

In *Give Me Liberty*, Gerry Spence, an American lawyer and author, states that "the people of a nation are enslaved when, together, they are helpless to institute effective change."[46] As the last millennium came to a close, I stood on the edge of despair as I witnessed the apparent helplessness among African people to institute change in their lives. My despair did not come from the perception that change could not be effected, but rather that there was so little evidence of any efforts toward positive, sustainable change. Africa seemed so busy putting out the fires of enormous, pressing issues that little or no strategic thinking was actually taking place.

I remembered, for example, the massive floods that swept the southern part of the continent in 2000. The havoc that it wrought on the lives of people already so miserably poor left me wondering if there was any reason to hope at all. And things only seemed to get worse. No sooner had the floods subsided than other parts of the continent began reeling from one of the worst droughts in recent decades. The drought was followed by a devastating famine that gripped several southern African countries.

No doubt, the environment poses one of the leading threats to Africa's efforts for survival. In addition to battling the problems created by a swelling population, the continent is locked in a fight against nature that is stretching it to the limits of its ability to serve the basic needs of its people.

Robert D. Kaplan, in his highly publicized article entitled "The Coming Anarchy," places the environment at the top of the list of threats to global stability. The political and strategic impact of overpopulation, widespread disease, deforestation and soil erosion, water depletion and air pollution will not only prompt mass migrations and incite group conflicts, but it will be the core foreign-policy challenge from which most others will emanate.[47]

Yet, despite the severity of the threat it poses, the environment is only one of many other "fires" being fought on the continent. As Abdul Mohammed of the InterAfrica Group stated in a speech at the symposium on the newly formed African Union:

> Our reality today is that just about everything that could go wrong is going wrong with us. Let us begin by facing the difficult realities of our continent: the fact that our economies are crippled by corruption and mismanagement, that organized crime has penetrated the highest levels of many governments, that many states are adopting the language of democracy and human rights only with the

greatest reluctance, and that African institutions are weak and incapable of delivering on their mandates. The HIV / AIDS pandemic is a survival issue not just for tens of millions of Africans, but also for some of our nations themselves....[48]

In confronting these enormous obstacles to Africa's forward strides, one could be tempted to throw his hands in the air and concede that there is no hope. Yet these very crises generate opportunities for positive change.

Finding Hope, Even in Tragedy

The logic of this thinking was driven home to me in 1998 when Kenya found itself flung into the international limelight with the bombing of the American embassy in Nairobi. For one brief moment, the world stopped and glanced over in our direction. For one brief moment, we were the front-page news. It didn't last long, but it made them look.

For those of us living in Kenya at the time, life came to a virtual standstill as news of the embassy attack filtered out of the city into the countryside. Things that had been so important just moments before the explosion suddenly took a back seat. Our lives, our priorities, were in one instant reorganized. The world responded to the incident with a spontaneous outpouring of sympathy for the bombing victims and their families. Politicians, churches, businesses, and ordinary people joined hands in an almost unprecedented show of national unity. Donations of money, food, and supplies were overwhelming.

Amidst the smoke and dust and blood, I glimpsed a new Africa rising up with a new resolve to feed her own poor, to care for her own sick, to lift up her own broken or disabled souls. I had a vision of what Africa could be. As a writer, I had an impulse to pick up my pen, and with the dust still settling around us, I sat down and wrote a commentary for Kenya's *Daily Nation*. The article was published two days after the embassy bombing and reflected my sorrow, but more significantly, this new hope that had been ignited in me:

> If anything positive can be found in the horrible bombing incident, it is that it served as a wake-up call to Kenyans, many of whom did not realize how much they love their country.... As we mourn with those who have lost their loved ones, let us not hide from the fact that this occurrence has in fact served to momentarily divert our attentions from some pretty serious issues facing this country....
>
> Many Kenyans have lost a sense of who they are and why they exist at all. If ever there was an opportunity for Kenyans to stop and change course, it is now....
>
> Out of the debris and ashes that remain of the horrible incident, a new nation has a chance to emerge. Out of this disaster, a new hope can be found for rebuilding the lost glory of Kenya. Let us not wait for another disaster to pull us together. Let us not slip back into the mire of hopelessness. Above all, let us not lose the opportunity to take what was meant for evil to turn it into good.[49]

Out of the tragedy of that bombing, I came to realize that I, as an individual, have no right to make demands of others to do something if I am not prepared to do my part. And so it is with my hope for positive change in Africa. The overall effort to turn this continent around will be the sum total of individual efforts—individuals like you and me—in our own little corners of this enormous and complex puzzle.

One Woman's Determination

In light of this truth, I would like to share the story of how one woman whom I had the privilege of knowing transformed the lives of some children in a way that no donor grant or government program could have achieved. The story begins on a Sunday morning sometime in early 1994 in the crowded compound of a large uptown church in Nairobi. Unnoticed by many of the faithful who were streaming into the church for the morning service, the wife of the pastor walked quietly to the main gate of the compound and handed out some sandwiches to a group of street children who had gathered outside, as usual on Sunday mornings, to peer at the affluent world within.

The children would never dare to enter the compound for fear of being beaten by the security guards who roamed the complex guarding the cars against break-ins. Many of those who sat in the pews each Sunday saw these children as a nuisance and a menace. The children were not only filthy-looking, but they seemed unruly and dangerous.

The children grabbed the few sandwiches that the woman offered and then ran off, bickering among themselves and creating an ugly scene. As she made her way slowly back toward the church, the pastor's wife resolved not to stand on the sidelines any longer. She decided that she would show these unwanted children the same love that her husband was preaching inside the church walls. It was the beginning of a crusade that would raise the eyebrows of many well-meaning people, who saw the growing problem of street children in Nairobi as being beyond what the church could handle.

From a logistical angle, the skepticism was quite valid. If word were to get around that the church was handing out free food on Sunday mornings, the church could find itself with a burden clearly beyond its capacity. Such an initiative would need careful planning, not to mention adequate facilities and manpower, neither of which the church had. Not surprisingly, the church board turned down the woman's request to allocate a budget for the activity. As much as they could sympathize with her cause, the board members could not, as the entrusted stewards, commit the church to take on such an ambitious program with its limited resources.

Dejected but undeterred, the woman decided to round up a handful of willing volunteers to help her in her quest to do something for these disadvantaged children. With the full support of her husband, she bought food and began to feed the children from their own resources.

She began gathering the children at a distant corner of the church compound where they would have their own little Sunday school class and their only hot meal of the week. The meetings gradually spilled into Mondays, and in the months to follow, the program would evolve into a daily gathering in which the children were provided with a few brief hours of respite from their miserable existence on the streets.

As support from well-wishers increased and the program picked up momentum, the church leadership came to see the results of the woman's determination. Funds were eventually allocated in the church budget for the activity, enabling the hiring of some full-time staff and the purchase of clothing, books, and other supplies.

Two years later I was among the hundreds of people who attended the opening of a wonderfully built facility that would serve as a home for up to one hundred homeless children. Most of the children who entered the center could neither read nor write. Many were addicted to glue and other drugs obtained on the streets. Through my own involvement with the center, I was able to witness the dramatic changes that took place in their young lives.

Each one of those children has a story that I hope will one day be told. But the bigger story is that of one determined woman, Sister Esther White, whose love for these children inspired her to take steps that would transform their lives.

Finding a New Focus

In his first bid for the White House, Bill Clinton's campaign team rallied around a simple slogan that is believed to be one of the key reasons for his victory. The slogan was "It's the economy, stupid!" The aim of the slogan was to keep the campaign focused on what Clinton aides considered to be the central issue and to avoid distractions by the opposition, the media, and the often misleading opinion polls. The slogan also served as a sieve through which new ideas and strategies were vetted.

We in Africa need a similar clarity of focus if we are to succeed in breaking the cycle of poverty and suffering on the continent. One such opportunity that has been presented to us is the New Partnership for African Development (NEPAD). NEPAD is a pledge by African leaders to place their countries, both individually and collectively, on a path of sustainable growth and development, and at the same time to participate actively in the world economy.

The NEPAD prospectus, which has been formally adopted by the African Union, speaks of a "new political will" among emerging African leadership. It presents an urgent action plan for development of the continent and outlines concrete steps to be taken at all levels—national, regional, and local—to create conditions for sustainable development.

One of the main objectives of NEPAD is to bring about an average GDP growth rate of not less than seven percent per annum in the next fifteen years. Another cardinal goal is to set a deadline of 2015 for meeting the following International Development Goals (IDGs), which were proposed at the United Nations Millennium Summit in 1995:

- reduce 1990 level of extreme poverty by half
- enroll all school-age children in schools
- reduce infant- and child-mortality rate by two-thirds
- reduce maternal maternity ratios by three-fourths
- provide universal access to reproductive services
- remove all gender disparities
- reverse loss of environmental resources by implementing national strategies for sustainable development

The success of NEPAD in meeting its current objectives is not as important as the direction and momentum it will trigger. There will be many challenges and obstacles along the way, and skepticism from the naysayers. But without a sustained focus on these strategic targets, Africa stands to suffer irreversible losses as it battles one catastrophe after another.

Needless to say, the population will continue to increase; droughts and floods will certainly come. Corruption and mismanagement of national resources will not disappear overnight. But a new track will have been laid for a new marathon. NEPAD provides both a springboard and a context for those of us who would *choose* to enter the race in earnest.

Choosing To Make a Difference

As surely as smallpox has been eliminated, so can malaria, tuberculosis, and AIDS. As surely as slavery was banished in North America and Europe, so can it be throughout Africa. As surely as the countries of western Europe have come to live in peace with one another, so can the countries of Africa. The endless conflicts and wars that dog the continent may have their roots in history, but they should not diminish the opportunity that we have today to choose a different course.

What our communities need are leaders who are willing to sacrifice their time and to invest their own resources. Our young people need role models who will show them the value of hard work, resourcefulness, integrity, and commitment. Every day is an opportunity to sow seeds that we will eventually reap.

If we sow seeds of discord, we must be prepared to accept a harvest of conflict. If we want to see a more caring and productive society, then we must look hard at ourselves in the mirror and ask what we can do to bring about that eventuality. We can write beautiful papers about development and pour money into large projects and massive institutions, but we must first change the way we think before practical solutions can begin to make any sense.

And now, I will show you an even more excellent way. Without genuine respect and *compassion* for people, hope becomes just another word in the dictionary. The message is so simple that it lends itself easily to ridicule. Yet who can escape the glare of its truth?

> *If I speak in the tongues of men and of angels, but have not love,*
> *I am only a resounding gong or clanging cymbal. If I have the*
> *gift of prophecy and can fathom all mysteries and all knowledge,*

and if I have faith that can move mountains, but have not love, I am nothing. If I give all I possess to the poor and surrender my body to the flames, but have not love, I gain nothing.

Love is patient; love is kind. It does not envy, it does not boast; it is not proud. It is not rude; it is not self-seeking; it is not easily angered; it keeps no record of wrongs. Love does not delight in evil but rejoices with the truth. It always protects, always trusts, always hopes, always perseveres.

Love never fails. But where there are prophecies, they will cease; where there are tongues, they will be stilled; where there is knowledge, it will pass away… And now these three remain: faith, hope, and love. But the greatest of these is love. [50]

Notes

[1]Stephen R. Covey, *The Seven Habits of Highly Effective People: Restoring the Character Ethic* (London: Simon & Schuster, 1992), 42.

[2]Poem by C. W. Longenecker

[3]C. Douglas Lummis, "The Myth Of Catch-Up Development" *Panos* (1 January 2000)

[4]*Time* (30 March 1998)

[5]Malegapuru W. Makgoba, ed., *African Renaissance: The New Struggle* (Sandton: Mafube/Tafelberg, 1999), xviii.

[6]*The Economist* (13 May 2000)

[7]*Stephen R. Covey, The Seven Habits of Highly Effective People: Restoring the Character Ethic* (London: Simon & Schuster, 1992), 22.

[8]Chudi Ukpabi, *Doing Business in Africa: Myths and Realities* (Amsterdam: Royal Tropical Institute, 1990), 18.

[9]"Trading Up," *The New Republic* (11 May 1998)

[10]Jeffrey D. Sachs, "Helping The World's Poorest," *The Economist* (14 August 1999)

[11]Robert Chambers, *Rural Development: Putting the Last First* (London: Longman, Inc., 1983) pp. 2

[12]Neely Tucker, Free Press Foreign Correspondent, "Aids Denial Ravages Africa—Conspiracy Theories Spread With Disease" (14 August 1999)

[13]*Ibid.*

[14] "AIDS: Africa's Top Killer," BBC News Online (12 May 1999)

[15]Charles L. Geshekter, "Reappraising Aids In Africa—Under-development and Racial Stereotypes," *Rethinking Aids*, vol. 5, no. 7 (September-October 1997)

[16]Bryan Ellison and Peter Duesberg, "The SMON Fiasco" (http// www.virussmith.net, 1996)

[17]Neville Hodgkinson, "Aids: Is Anyone Positive?" *The European* (22 June 1998)

[18]Neville Hodgkinson, "Conspiracy Of Silence," *Sunday Times* (London, 3 April 1994)

[19]*Sunday Times* (London, 17 May 1992)

[20]Charles L. Geshekter, "Reappraising Aids In Africa—Under-Development and Racial Stereotypes," *Rethinking Aids*, vol. 5,

no. 7 (September-October 1997)

[21]Eleni Papadopulos-Eleoulos and Valendar Turner, "Aids in Africa," *Rethinking AIDS* (January 1995)

[22]*International Herald Tribune* (20 June 2002)

[23]Charles L. Geshekter, "Reappraising Aids In Africa—Under-development and Racial Stereotypes," *Rethinking Aids*, vol. 5, no. 7 (September-October 1997)

[24]Salih Booker, "The Myth of HIPC Debt Relief," *The Mail& Guardian* (12 December 2000)

[25]"Putting Life Before Debt," Catholic Church Statement, *CIDSE and Caritas Internationalis*

[26]Yoweri K. Museveni, "What is Africa's Problem?" (Kampala: NRM Publications, 1992), 20.

[27]*Washington Post* (30 April 2001)

[28]Malegapuru W. Makgoba, ed., *African Renaissance: The New Struggle* (Sandton: Mafube/Tafelberg, 1999), 62.

[29]"Scramble for Africa," *The Economist* (7 December 2000)

[30]Colin Blane, BBC Report, "Belgian Wealth Squeezed from Congo" (18 January 2001)

[31]"In the Heart of Darkness," *The Economist* (7 December 2000)

[32]Basil Davidson, *The Black Man's Burden: Africa and the Curse of the Nation State* (Oxford: James Currey Ltd., 1992), 219.

[33]UNDP, 1996 Human Development Report

[34]U. S. Committee for Refugees, Refugee Reports, vol. 21, no. 7 (2000)

[35]Tunde Obadina, "Slave Trade: A Route to African Contemporary Crisis," *Africa Business Information Services* (2000)

[36]Tunde Obadina, "The Myth of Neo-Colonialism," *Africa Business Information Services* (2001)

[37]Pauline Muchina, "The Economic Deterioration and the Debt Crisis in Africa: A Theological Response," article written for *Women in Ministry* web page.

[38]Keith B. Richburg, *Out of America — A Black Man Confronts Africa* (San Diego: Harcourt Brace & Company, 1998), 233.

[39]Ryan Lizza, "Where Angels Fear to Tread," *The New Republic*

(24 July 2000)

[40]David C. Korten, *When Corporations Rule the World* (West Hartford, Connecticut: Kumarian Press/Berrett-Koehler, 1995), 39.

[41]*Ibid.*, 54.

[42]Walter Rodney, *How Europe Underdeveloped Africa* (Nairobi: East African Educational Publishers, 1989), 34.

[43]*The Economist* (11 August 2000)

[44]David C. Korten, *When Corporations Rule the World* (West Hartford, Connecticut: Kumarian Press/Berrett-Koehler, 1995), 5.

[45]Yoweri K. Museveni, "What is Africa's Problem?" (Kampala: NRM Publications, 1992), 9.

[46]Gerry Spence, *Give me Liberty: Freeing Ourselves in the Twenty-First Century* (New York: St. Martin's Griffin, 1998), 8.

[47]Robert D. Kaplan, "The Coming Anarchy," *Atlantic Monthly* (February 1994)

[48]Abdul Mohammed, "Challenges for the Africa Union," keynote presentation at the symposium on the African Union, Addis Ababa (3 March 2002)

[49]Pete Ondeng, "Dare One Hope for Good Out of Bomb Nightmare?," *Daily Nation* (10 August 1998)

[50]*The Bible*, New International Version (NIV), I Corinthians 13.

About the Author

Pete Ondeng is widely known and respected in his native Kenya as the author of *How To Start Your Own Small Business* and as a former columnist for the Daily Nation. As an entrepreneur and specialist in economic development, he has acquired over twenty years of experience in both the private and public sectors. As a U. S. certified public accountant (CPA), he started his career as an auditor with a Fortune 500 company. He later worked for USAID before assuming leadership of Faulu Kenya, one of the country's foremost microfinance institutions.

Ondeng returned to his beloved Kenya in July 2002 after four years in the Netherlands as the Africa Project support officer for Oikocredit, one of the world's largest private "wholesale" development finance intermediaries. Ondeng has chosen to return home to be part of the solution and currently serves as Chief Executive of the New Partnership for Africa's Development (NEPAD) Eastern Africa Secretariat.

Married with two sons, Ondeng resides in Nairobi.